KETCHUP VOCA

LEVEL 3 2

i-Scream edu

영어 공부의 핵심은 단어입니다.

케챱보카로
영어 단어 실력을 키우고,
상위 1% 어휘력을
따라잡아 보세요!

케챱보카 친구들

Dennis
엉뚱하고 낙천적인 성격의 자유로운 영혼!
예측 불가에, 공부에도 관심이 없지만,
운이 좋아 뭘 해도 잘 풀린대요.

Rod
인내심이 크고 생각도 깊은, 다정다감 엄친아!
개구쟁이 쌍둥이 누나, 애완묘 루나가 있어
혼자 있는 것보단 함께 하는 것을 좋아해요.

Kiara
노래를 좋아하는 사교성의 아이콘!
솔직하고 모든 일에 적극적이지만,
금방 사랑에 빠지는 짝사랑 전문가래요.

Sally
논리적이고 긍정적인 모범생!
친구들과 장난도 많이 치지만, 호기심이 많아
관심 분야에 다양한 지식을 갖고 있어요.

Mong
친구들이 궁금한 것이 있을 때 나타나는 해결사!
너무 아는 것이 많아서 어느 별에서 왔는지
궁금하기도 해요.

만화 스토리
친구들의 좌충우돌 일상이 그려진
재미있는 만화를 보며
단어 뜻을 배우고,
문장에 어떻게 활용되는지
알아볼 수 있어요!

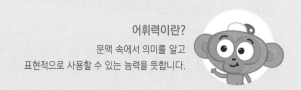

문맥 속에서 의미를 알고
표현적으로 사용할 수 있는 능력을 뜻합니다.

Know **Exercise** **Think** **Check** **Habit**

KETCH UP

망각 제로 단어 기억하기 습관으로
기억 장기화

게임으로 즐겁게 리뷰하고 테스트로 더블 체크

만화 스토리 〉 단어 〉 문장 순으로
단어 의미를 이해하며 모국어처럼 습득

이미지 연상 쓰기 연습으로 실제 단어 활용, 적용

주제별로 초등 필수 & 고난도 단어 학습하며
상위 1% 단어 마스터

KETCHUP
makes you Catch up.

How to Use

체계적인 4 Steps 시스템으로 학습 완성!

	Step 1	Step 2	Step 3	Step 4
Day 1~4				
Day 5				

Step 1

Warm up 망각 제로 & 스토리 단어 이해로 학습 준비하기

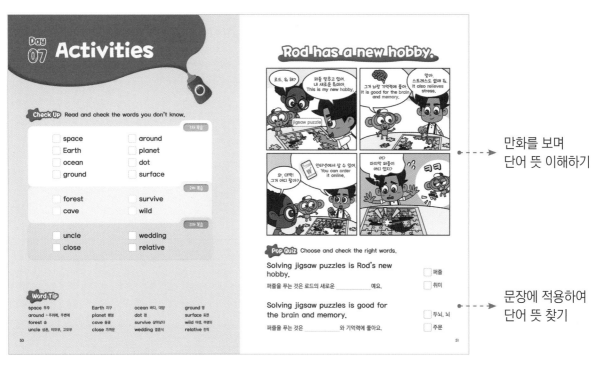

만화를 보며
단어 뜻 이해하기

문장에 적용하여
단어 뜻 찾기

※ 망각 제로는 p10에서 확인하세요!

Catch up 듣고, 말하고, 읽고, 쓰며, 상위 1% 단어 따라잡기

QR 찍어 단어 듣고 따라 말하기 ▶ 케찹병을 색칠하며 3번 반복하기

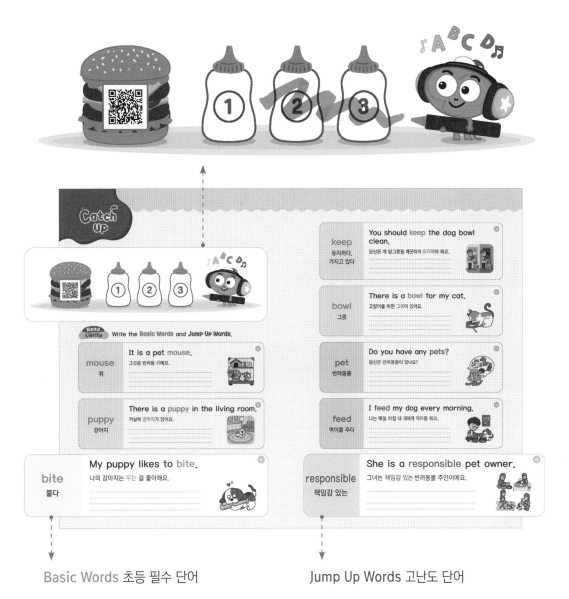

Basic Words 초등 필수 단어   Jump Up Words 고난도 단어

품사 기호

v	verb (동사)	**adv**	adverb (부사)	**conj**	conjunction (접속사)
n	noun (명사)	**prep**	preposition (전치사)	**pron**	pronoun (대명사)
a	adjective (형용사)	**det**	determiner (한정사)	**num**	numeral (수사)

케찹보카와 함께
상위 1% CATCH UP!

Step 3

Skill up 두뇌 자극 이미지 연상 학습으로 실력 강화하기

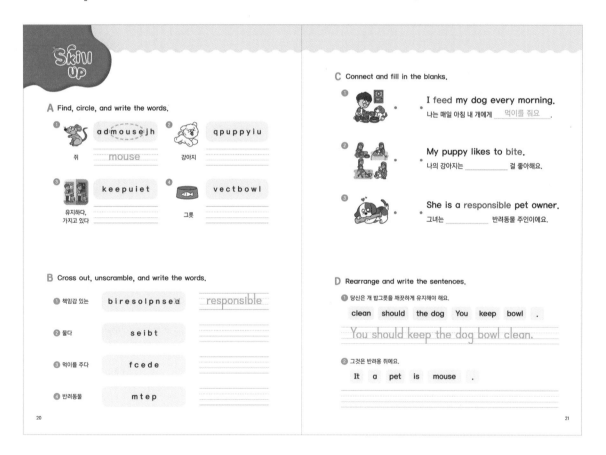

Skill UP

A Find, circle, and write the words.

① admousejh
쥐   mouse

② qpuppyiu
강아지

③ keepuiet
유지하다,
가지고 있다

④ vectbowl
그릇

B Cross out, unscramble, and write the words.

① 책임감 있는   biresolpnsed   responsible

② 물다   seibt

③ 먹이를 주다   fcede

④ 반려동물   mtep

C Connect and fill in the blanks.

① I feed my dog every morning.
나는 매일 아침 내 개에게 ___먹이를 줘요___.

② My puppy likes to bite.
나의 강아지는 _____ 걸 좋아해요.

③ She is a responsible pet owner.
그녀는 _____ 반려동물 주인이에요.

D Rearrange and write the sentences.

① 당신은 개 밥그릇을 깨끗하게 유지해야 해요.

clean should the dog You keep bowl .

You should keep the dog bowl clean.

② 그것은 반려용 쥐예요.

It a pet is mouse .

20   21

유형 1	유형 2	유형 3	유형 4
이미지 연상을 통해 단어 완성하기	우리말에 맞춰 스펠링 배열하여 단어 쓰기	이미지와 문장을 연결하여 단어 뜻 이해하기	배운 단어 적용하여 문장 완성하여 쓰기

Wrap up 게임과 최종 평가를 통해 단어 학습 마무리하기

쉬어가기

다양한 유형의 재미있는 게임하며 단어 복습하기!

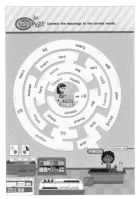

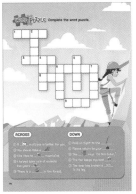

Word Maze
알맞은 스펠링으로 이뤄진
단어를 따라가
미로 찾기

Word Puzzle
주어진 문장에
알맞은 단어를 쓰며
퍼즐 완성하기

Word Search 1
힌트를 보고
알맞은 그림을 찾아
쓰기 연습하기

Word Search 2
다양한 알파벳 속
배운 단어를 찾아
쓰기 연습하기

복습&테스트

지금까지 배운 단어 정리하고, 테스트로 최종 점검!
뜯어서 쓰는 나만의 단어장까지!

7

Study Planner & Contents

FINISH

Part I

START

Day 01 History

망각 제로란?

> 망각 제로는
> 학습 주기를 활용해서 복습하는 거야.

> 지난번에 공부했던 단어 중에
> 아는 것과 모르는 것을 확인해 볼 수 있겠네!

Day 07 Activities

Check Up Read and check the words you don't know.

1차 복습

- [ ] space
- [ ] Earth
- [ ] ocean
- [ ] ground
- [ ] around
- [ ] planet
- [ ] dot
- [ ] surface

2차 복습

- [ ] forest
- [ ] cave
- [ ] survive
- [ ] wild

3차 복습

- [ ] uncle
- [ ] close
- [ ] wedding
- [ ] relative

Word Tip

space 우주	Earth 지구	ocean 바다, 대양	ground 땅
~~nd - 주위에, 주변에~~	planet 행성	dot 점	surface 표면
~~st 숲~~	cave 동굴	survive 살아남다	wild 야생, 야생의
			relative 친척

Check Up

복습 주기에 맞춰 반복 학습하기

1차 복습	1일 전 공부한 단어
2차 복습	3일 전 공부한 단어
3차 복습	7일 전 공부한 단어

Pop Quiz Choose and check the right words.

Solving jigsaw puzzles is Rod's new hobby.
퍼즐을 푸는 것은 로드의 새로운 _____ 예요.
- [ ] 퍼즐
- [ ] 취미

Solving jigsaw puzzles is good for the brain and memory.
퍼즐을 푸는 것은 _____ 와 기억력에 좋아요.
- [ ] 두뇌, 뇌
- [ ] 주문

51

Word Tip

정확한 단어 뜻 확인하기

" 우리 같이
망각 제로 학습해 보자 "

※ 망각 제로는 [DAY 02]부터 시작합니다.

What will the 22nd century be like?

Choose and check the right words.

Sally wonders what the 22nd century will be like.

샐리는 22_____는 어떨지 궁금해요.

- ✓ 세기
- ☐ 대학

Sally will use glass cups from now on.

샐리는 지금부터 _____컵을 사용할 거예요.

- ☐ 유리
- ☐ 평화

11

 Write the **Basic Words** and **Jump Up Words**.

| history 역사 | **I am good at history.**
 나는 역사를 잘 알아요.

 history | n |

| last 지속되다 | **The war lasted for many years.**
 그 전쟁은 여러 해 동안 지속되었어요. | v |

| peace 평화 | **This organization works for peace.**
 이 조직은 평화를 위해 일해요. | n |

college
대학

This college was founded in 1936. _n_

이 대학은 1936년에 설립되었어요.

---

glass
유리

This building is made of glass. _n_

이 건물은 유리로 만들어졌어요.

---

century
세기, 100년

A century is one hundred years. _n_

한 세기는 100년이에요.

1700 1800 1900 2000

---

modern
현대적인, 현대의

Seoul is a modern city. _a_

서울은 현대적인 도시예요.

---

provide
제공하다, 주다

She provided a tour of the museum. _v_

그녀는 박물관 투어를 제공했어요.

A Choose and write the words.

history	college	century

1

1700 1800 1900 2000

century

세기, 100년

2

역사

3

대학

B Choose and write the words.

provide	modern	peace	glass

1 평화   peace

2 제공하다, 주다

3 유리

4 현대적인, 현대의

14

C Unscramble and complete the sentences.

1 그 전쟁은 여러 해 동안 지속되었어요.

a t l s e d

The war ___lasted___ for many years.

2 이 건물은 유리로 만들어졌어요.

l s s g a

This building is made of _____.

3 서울은 현대적인 도시예요.

m r e n d o

Seoul is a _____ city.

D Choose and complete the sentences.

history   century   college

1 한 세기는 100년이에요.

A ___century___ is one hundred years.

2 나는 역사를 잘 알아요.

I am good at _____.

3 이 대학은 1936년에 설립되었어요.

This _____ was founded in 1936.

Day 02 Jobs

Check Up Read and check the words you don't know.

1차 복습

- [ ] history
- [ ] last
- [ ] peace
- [ ] college
- [ ] glass
- [ ] century
- [ ] modern
- [ ] provide

※ **망각 제로!** 1일 전 학습한 단어를 복습해요.

Word Tip

history 역사	last 지속되다	peace 평화	college 대학
glass 유리	century 세기, 100년	modern 현대적인, 현대의	provide 제공하다, 주다

What does Dennis want to be?

데니스는 아직 장래 희망을 정하지 못했어요.

난 미래에 무엇이 되고 싶은지 모르겠어.
I don't know what I want to be in the future.

기술자는 어때?
How about becoming an engineer?

글쎄....

요리사도 멋있겠어!

chef

먹는 것은 자신 있는데!

교수도 멋있을 것 같아!
You'd be a good professor!

지루할 거 같아....

아무래도 투명 인간이 제일 재밌겠어.

Pop Quiz Choose and check the right words.

Dennis doesn't know what he wants to be in the future.

데니스는 _____에 무엇이 되고 싶은지 몰라요.

- [ ] 미래
- [ ] 변호사

Kiara thinks that Dennis would be a good professor.

키아라는 데니스가 _____가 되면 멋있을 것 같다고 생각해요.

- [ ] 요리사
- [ ] 교수

17

 **Listen & Say** Listen, say, and color.

① ② ③

Read & Write Write the **Basic Words** and **Jump Up Words**.

future 미래	**I want to be a pilot in the future.** (n) 나는 미래에 조종사가 되고 싶어요.

become ~이 되다	**I will become a film director.** (v) 나는 영화감독이 될 거예요.

wish 바라다, 원하다	**We all wish for good jobs.** (v) 우리는 모두 좋은 직업을 바라요.

engineer
기술자

The engineer **is designing a new machine.**

그 기술자는 새 기계를 설계하고 있어요.

---

library
도서관

He works at a library**.**

그는 도서관에서 일해요.

---

professor
교수

I want to be a professor**.**

나는 교수가 되고 싶어요.

---

chef
요리사

He is a world-famous chef**.**

그는 세계적으로 유명한 요리사예요.

---

lawyer
변호사

He studied for a long time to be a lawyer**.**

그는 변호사가 되기 위해 오랫동안 공부했어요.

A Find, circle, and write the words.

1 미래

(f u t u r e) j h

future

2 ~이 되다

q u b e c o m e

3 바라다, 원하다

k w i s h h e t

4 변호사

e l a w y e r a

B Cross out, unscramble, and write the words.

1 도서관

l b a r r y i ✗

2 요리사

s c f e h

3 기술자

r g e n i n e e a

4 교수

r o r o p m f s s e

C Connect and fill in the blanks.

1

I want to be a professor.

나는 _____교수_____가 되고 싶어요.

2

He is a world-famous chef.

그는 세계적으로 유명한 _____예요.

3

He works at a library.

그는 _____에서 일해요.

D Rearrange and write the sentences.

1 우리는 모두 좋은 직업을 바라요.

| wish | good | for | all | We | jobs | . |

We all wish for good jobs.

2 나는 영화감독이 될 거예요.

| I | film director | a | become | will | . |

Day 03 Travel

Check Up Read and check the words you don't know.

- ☐ future
- ☐ become
- ☐ wish
- ☐ engineer
- ☐ library
- ☐ professor
- ☐ chef
- ☐ lawyer

※ **망각 제로!** 1일 전 학습한 단어를 복습해요.

Word Tip

future 미래

become ~이 되다

wish 바라다, 원하다

engineer 기술자

library 도서관

professor 교수

chef 요리사

lawyer 변호사

Let's go on a trip.

Pop Quiz Choose and check the right words.

The sky is clear and blue.

하늘이 ＿＿＿＿＿＿＿＿ 파래요.

- [ ] 현대적인
- [ ] 맑은

Dennis's family is ready to leave.

데니스의 가족은 떠날 ＿＿＿＿＿＿＿＿요.

- [ ] 준비가 된
- [ ] 곧

23

 Listen, say, and color.

 Write the Basic Words and Jump Up Words.

We went on a tour of France.

tour
여행, 관광

우리는 프랑스로 여행을 떠났어요.

Don't forget your sunscreen!

forget
잊다

선크림 챙기는 것 잊지 마세요!

We flew on a clear day.

clear
맑은, 깨끗한

우리는 맑은 날에 비행기를 타고 떠났어요.

hurry

서두르다

Hurry up, or we'll miss the bus. (v)

서둘러요, 그렇지 않으면 버스를 놓칠 거예요.

---

ready

준비가 된

The airplane is ready for takeoff. (a)

그 비행기는 이륙 준비가 되었어요.

---

passport

여권

May I see your passport? (n)

여권 좀 보여주시겠어요?

---

soon

곧, 머지않아

Our summer vacation will end soon. (adv)

우리의 여름 방학이 곧 끝날 거예요.

---

delay

지연하다,
미루다

The plane was delayed because of fog. (v)

비행기는 안개 때문에 지연되었어요.

A Choose and write the words.

delay	soon	passport

1

_____
_____
_____

여권

2

09:30
Time Gate Status
09:00 17 DELAYED

_____
_____
_____

지연하다, 미루다

3

SUN MON TUE WED THU FRI SAT
1 2 3 4 5 6 7
8 9 10 11 12 13 14
15 16 17 18 19 20 21
22 23 24 25 26 27 28
29 30 31
vacation
Today

_____
_____
_____

곧, 머지않아

B Choose and write the words.

hurry	ready	forget	tour

1 준비가 된

_____   _____

2 잊다

_____   _____

3 서두르다

_____   _____

4 여행, 관광

_____   _____

C Connect and fill in the blanks.

1

We went on a tour of France.

우리는 프랑스로 _____을 떠났어요.

2

Don't forget your sunscreen!

선크림 챙기는 것 _____ 마세요!

3

We flew on a clear day.

우리는 _____ 날에 비행기를 타고 떠났어요.

D Rearrange and write the sentences.

1 여권 좀 보여주시겠어요?

| see | May | I | passport | your | ? |

_____

- -

_____

2 우리의 여름 방학이 곧 끝날 거예요.

| end | Our | will | soon | summer vacation | . |

_____

- -

_____

Day 04 Daily Routines

Check Up Read and check the words you don't know.

1차 복습

☐ tour
☐ forget
☐ clear
☐ hurry

☐ ready
☐ passport
☐ soon
☐ delay

2차 복습

☐ history
☐ last

☐ modern
☐ provide

※ **망각 제로!** 1일 전 3일 전 학습한 단어를 복습해요.

Word Tip

tour 여행, 관광	**forget** 잊다	**clear** 맑은, 깨끗한	**hurry** 서두르다
ready 준비가 된	**passport** 여권	**soon** 곧, 머지않아	**delay** 지연하다, 미루다
history 역사	**last** 지속되다	**modern** 현대적인, 현대의	**provide** 제공하다, 주다

Kiara wants to have straight hair.

Pop Quiz Choose and check the right words.

Kiara's hair is curlier on wet days.

키아라의 머리카락은 _____ 날에 더 곱슬거려요.

- [ ] 건조한
- [ ] 젖은

After Kiara took a bath, her hair was curly again.

- [ ] 목욕
- [ ] 비밀

_____ 후에, 키아라의 머리카락은 다시 곱슬거렸어요.

dry 마르다, 건조한	**My T-shirt will dry in the sun.** 내 티셔츠는 햇볕에서 마를 거예요. _____ _____ _____	v a 

wet 젖은	**My cat got wet in the rain.** 내 고양이가 비에 젖었어요. _____ _____ _____	a

decide 결정하다	**He decided to go home early.** 그는 집에 일찍 가기로 결정했어요. _____ _____ _____	v

shock
충격을 주다,
충격

I was shocked to hear the news. (v) (n)

나는 그 소식을 듣고 충격을 받았어요.

_____
- -
_____

bath
목욕, 욕조

I take a bath before bed. (n)

나는 자기 전에 목욕해요.

_____
- -
_____

apply
바르다, 신청하다

Apply the lotion to your face. (v)

로션을 얼굴에 바르세요.

_____
- -
_____

secret
비밀, 비결

We promised to keep the secret. (n)

우리는 비밀을 지키기로 약속했어요.

_____
- -
_____

strange
이상한, 낯선

He wears strange pajamas to bed. (a)

그는 이상한 잠옷을 입고 잠자리에 들어요.

_____
- -
_____

A Choose and write the words.

shock	decide	apply

1

_____

결정하다

2

_____

충격을 주다, 충격

3

_____

바르다, 신청하다

B Choose and write the words.

strange	dry	bath	wet

1 이상한, 낯선

_____   _____

2 마르다, 건조한

_____   _____

3 젖은

_____   _____

4 목욕, 욕조

_____   _____

C Unscramble and complete the sentences.

1 내 고양이가 비에 젖었어요.　　　　　　t e w

My cat got _____ in the rain.

2 우리는 비밀을 지키기로 약속했어요.　　e c r t s e

We promised to keep the _____.

3 나는 자기 전에 목욕해요.　　　　　　t h a b

I take a _____ before bed.

D Choose and complete the sentences.

Apply　　　　shocked　　　　decided

1 나는 그 소식을 듣고 충격을 받았어요.

I was _____ to hear the news.

2 그는 집에 일찍 가기로 결정했어요.

He _____ to go home early.

3 로션을 얼굴에 바르세요.

_____ the lotion to your face.

Day 05 Following Directions

Check UP Read and check the words you don't know.

1차 복습

- [ ] dry
- [ ] wet
- [ ] decide
- [ ] shock

- [ ] bath
- [ ] apply
- [ ] secret
- [ ] strange

2차 복습

- [ ] future
- [ ] become

- [ ] chef
- [ ] lawyer

※ **망각 제로!** 1일 전 3일 전 학습한 단어를 복습해요.

 Word Tip

dry 마르다, 건조한
bath 목욕, 욕조
future 미래

wet 젖은
apply 바르다, 신청하다
become ~이 되다

decide 결정하다
secret 비밀, 비결
chef 요리사

shock 충격을 주다, 충격
strange 이상한, 낯선
lawyer 변호사

Rod is left-handed.

Pop Quiz Choose and check the right words.

Dennis holds scissors with his left hand.

데니스는 _____ 손으로 가위를 잡았어요.

☐ 오른쪽
☐ 왼쪽

Public places are sometimes inconvenient for Rod.

로드는 때때로 _____ 장소에서 불편해요.

☐ 공공의
☐ 무작위의

left 왼쪽으로, 왼쪽의	**Go straight and turn left.** adv a 쭉 가서 왼쪽으로 도세요. _____ - _____	

right 오른쪽으로, 오른쪽의	**Go straight and turn right.** adv a 쭉 가서 오른쪽으로 도세요. _____ - _____	

above ~보다 위에	**Hang the picture above the couch.** prep 소파 위에 그림을 걸어 놓으세요. _____ - _____	

hold
잡고 있다, 잡다

Hold **on tight.**
꽉 잡으세요.

v

---

now
지금, 이제

Start writing now.
지금부터 쓰기 시작하세요.

adv

---

random
무작위의

Pick a random **card from this hat.**
이 모자에서 무작위로 카드를 고르세요.

a

---

public
공공의,
대중을 위한

Please do not litter in public **areas.**
공공장소에 쓰레기를 버리지 마세요.

a

---

spin
돌다, 회전하다

Spin the wheel!
휠을 돌려요!

v

A Find, circle, and write the words.

1 왼쪽으로, 왼쪽의

o l o w l e f t

_____

2 오른쪽으로, 오른쪽의

t r i g h t q a

_____

3 ~보다 위에

a b o v e u e t

_____

4 잡고 있다, 잡다

c h o l d e y z

_____

B Cross out, unscramble, and write the words.

1 지금, 이제

w n s o

_____

2 무작위의

a d m r l o n

_____

3 공공의, 대중을 위한

u b p c l i h

_____

4 돌다, 회전하다

s p q n i

_____

C Connect and fill in the blanks.

1

Spin the wheel!

휠을 _____!

2

Please do not litter in public areas.

_____장소에 쓰레기를 버리지 마세요.

3

Start writing now.

_____부터 쓰기 시작하세요.

D Rearrange and write the sentences.

1 꽉 잡으세요.

on   tight   Hold   .

_____

2 쭉 가서 왼쪽으로 도세요.

straight   Go   and   left   turn   .

_____

WORD SEARCH
Find, circle, and write the words.

Words go in 2 directions → ↓

h	l	h	t	c	x	u	d	d	w
m	b	a	t	h	l	k	q	r	q
g	c	x	r	i	g	h	t	m	v
l	f	q	c	j	k	r	t	k	l
e	u	c	e	q	p	l	a	s	t
f	t	l	n	r	o	w	b	z	u
t	u	e	t	g	r	e	k	t	w
v	r	a	u	o	v	t	v	o	i
r	r	e	r	k	d	t	a	u	s
y	i	p	y	p	p	y	i	v	r	h

Word Bank
last • wish
century • bath
future • tour
clear • wet
right • left

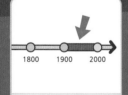

century

history 역사	**last** 지속되다	**peace** 평화	**college** 대학	**glass** 유리
century 세기, 100년	**modern** 현대적인, 현대의	**provide** 제공하다, 주다	**future** 미래	**become** ~이 되다
wish 바라다, 원하다	**engineer** 기술자	**library** 도서관	**professor** 교수	**chef** 요리사
lawyer 변호사	**tour** 여행, 관광	**forget** 잊다	**clear** 맑은, 깨끗한	**hurry** 서두르다
ready 준비가 된	**passport** 여권	**soon** 곧, 머지않아	**delay** 지연하다, 미루다	**dry** 마르다, 건조한
wet 젖은	**decide** 결정하다	**shock** 충격을 주다, 충격	**bath** 목욕, 욕조	**apply** 바르다, 신청하다
secret 비밀, 비결	**strange** 이상한, 낯선	**left** 왼쪽으로, 왼쪽의	**right** 오른쪽으로, 오른쪽의	**above** ~보다 위에
hold 잡고 있다, 잡다	**now** 지금, 이제	**random** 무작위의	**public** 공공의, 대중을 위한	**spin** 돌다, 회전하다

#

맞힌 개수 : ⬚ / 40

영어		한국어	
① history		㉑ 유리	
② last		㉒ 세기, 100년	
③ peace		㉓ 현대적인, 현대의	
④ college		㉔ 제공하다, 주다	
⑤ future		㉕ 도서관	
⑥ become		㉖ 교수	
⑦ wish		㉗ 요리사	
⑧ engineer		㉘ 변호사	
⑨ tour		㉙ 준비가 된	
⑩ forget		㉚ 여권	
⑪ clear		㉛ 곧, 머지않아	
⑫ hurry		㉜ 지연하다, 미루다	
⑬ dry		㉝ 목욕, 욕조	
⑭ wet		㉞ 바르다, 신청하다	
⑮ decide		㉟ 비밀, 비결	
⑯ shock		㊱ 이상한, 낯선	
⑰ left		㊲ 지금, 이제	
⑱ right		㊳ 무작위의	
⑲ above		㊴ 공공의, 대중을 위한	
⑳ hold		㊵ 돌다, 회전하다	

Part 2

FINISH

START

Day 06 People

1차 복습

- [ ] left
- [ ] right
- [ ] above
- [ ] hold
- [ ] now
- [ ] random
- [ ] public
- [ ] spin

2차 복습

- [ ] tour
- [ ] forget
- [ ] soon
- [ ] delay

※ **망각 제로!** 1일 전 3일 전 학습한 단어를 복습해요.

Word Tip

left 왼쪽으로, 왼쪽의	**right** 오른쪽으로, 오른쪽의	**above** ~보다 위에	**hold** 잡고 있다, 잡다
now 지금, 이제	**random** 무작위의	**public** 공공의, 대중을 위한	**spin** 돌다, 회전하다
tour 여행, 관광	**forget** 잊다	**soon** 곧, 머지않아	**delay** 지연하다, 미루다

44

Rod is good at giving speeches.

로드는 발표를 잘해요.
Rod is good at giving speeches.

난 발표할 때 목소리가 떨려.
My voice shakes when I speak in public.

오..오늘 바발표 할 내..내용은..

많은 사람들이 발표 불안이 있대.
Many people have public speaking anxiety.

발표를 잘하는 비결이 뭐야?

연습을 충분히 하고, 발표 전에 화장실도 가면 도움이 될 거야.

restroom

고마워!

PoP Quiz Choose and check the right words.

Rod is good at giving speeches.

로드는 _____ 을 잘해요.

☐ 농담
☐ 연설

Many people have public speaking anxiety.

많은 사람들이 발표 _____ 이 있어요.

☐ 불안
☐ 목소리

Catch Up

Listen, say, and color.

Read & Write Write the **Basic Words** and **Jump Up Words**.

---

voice
목소리

She has a lovely voice.

그녀는 매력적인 목소리를 가지고 있어요.

_____

_____

ⓝ

---

present
참석한, 있는

Many people were present at the meeting.

많은 사람들이 그 회의에 참석했어요.

_____

_____

ⓐ

---

restroom
화장실

Where is the nearest restroom?

가장 가까운 화장실이 어디에 있나요?

_____

_____

ⓝ

46

humor
유머, 농담

He has a good sense of humor. (n)

그는 유머 감각이 뛰어나요.

_____

_____

_____

many
많은

She has many candies in the basket. (det)

그녀는 바구니 안에 많은 사탕을 가지고 있어요.

_____

_____

_____

speech
연설, 담화

I was bored with his speech. (n)

나는 그의 연설이 지루했어요.

_____

_____

_____

pregnant
임신한

His wife is pregnant. (a)

그의 아내는 임신 중이에요.

_____

_____

_____

anxiety
불안(감)

I felt anxiety about my first day of school. (n)

나는 첫 등교일에 대해 불안감을 느꼈어요.

_____

_____

_____

A Choose and write the words.

pregnant	anxiety	speech

①
 _____
 임신한

②
 _____
 연설, 담화

③
 _____
 불안(감)

B Choose and write the words.

present	humor	restroom	many

① 많은 _____ _____

② 화장실 _____ _____

③ 유머, 농담 _____ _____

④ 참석한, 있는 _____ _____

C Connect and fill in the blanks.

1.
He has a good sense of humor.

그는 _____ 감각이 뛰어나요.

2.
She has a lovely voice.

그녀는 매력적인 _____를 가지고 있어요.

3.
Where is the nearest restroom?

가장 가까운 _____이 어디에 있나요?

D Rearrange and write the sentences.

1. 그의 아내는 임신 중이에요.

His   pregnant   is   wife   .

_____

_____

_____

2. 나는 그의 연설이 지루했어요.

I   with   speech   was   his   bored   .

_____

_____

_____

Day 07 Nature

Check Up Read and check the words you don't know.

1차 복습

- [ ] voice
- [ ] present
- [ ] restroom
- [ ] humor
- [ ] many
- [ ] speech
- [ ] pregnant
- [ ] anxiety

2차 복습

- [ ] dry
- [ ] wet
- [ ] secret
- [ ] strange

3차 복습

- [ ] peace
- [ ] college
- [ ] glass
- [ ] century

※ 망각 제로! 1일 전 3일 전 7일 전 학습한 단어를 복습해요.

Word Tip

voice 목소리	present 참석한, 있는	restroom 화장실	humor 유머, 농담
many 많은	speech 연설, 담화	pregnant 임신한	anxiety 불안(감)
dry 마르다, 건조한	wet 젖은	secret 비밀, 비결	strange 이상한, 낯선
peace 평화	college 대학	glass 유리	century 세기, 100년

How can I use a compass?

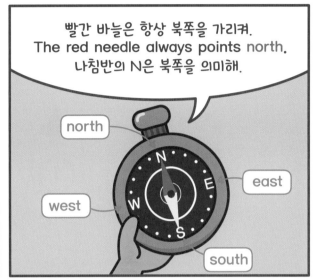

Pop Quiz Choose and check the right words.

The red needle always points north.

빨간 바늘은 항상 _____을 가리켜요.

☐ 북쪽
☐ 남쪽

The sun rises in the east.

해는 _____에서 떠요.

☐ 동쪽
☐ 서쪽

 Write the **Basic Words** and **Jump Up Words**.

east 동쪽	**The sun rises in the east.** 해는 동쪽에서 떠요.

west 서쪽	**The sun sets in the west.** 해는 서쪽으로 져요.

south 남쪽	**Birds fly to the south.** 새들이 남쪽으로 날아가요. 

north
북쪽

Penguins swim to the north. (n)

펭귄들이 북쪽으로 수영해요.

---

bottom
맨 아래 (부분), 바닥

The bottom of the ocean is cold. (n)

바다의 맨 아래 온도는 차가워요.

4°C

---

rise
뜨다, 오르다

Stars rise in the east, except for Polaris. (v)

북극성을 제외하고, 별들은 동쪽에서 떠요.

---

overhead
머리 위로, 머리 위의

A pigeon passed low overhead. (adv) (a)

비둘기 한 마리가 머리 위로 낮게 지나갔어요.

---

likely
~할 것 같은

It is likely to rain today. (a)

오늘은 비가 올 것 같아요.

A Choose and write the words.

bottom	overhead	likely

1

_____
- - - - - - - - - - - - - -
_____

맨 아래 (부분), 바닥

2

_____
- - - - - - - - - - - - - -
_____

머리 위로, 머리 위의

3

_____
- - - - - - - - - - - - - -
_____

~할 것 같은

B Choose and write the words.

south	west	east	north

1 동쪽

2 서쪽

3 남쪽

4 북쪽

54

C Unscramble and complete the sentences.

1 새들이 남쪽으로 날아가요.　　　t h s u o

Birds fly to the _____.

2 펭귄들이 북쪽으로 수영해요.　　　n o h t r

Penguins swim to the _____.

3 북극성을 제외하고, 별들은 동쪽에서 떠요.　　　s r e i

Stars _____ in the east, except for Polaris.

D Choose and complete the sentences.

overhead　　　east　　　west

1 해는 서쪽으로 져요.

The sun sets in the _____.

2 해는 동쪽에서 떠요.

The sun rises in the _____.

3 비둘기 한 마리가 머리 위로 낮게 지나갔어요.

A pigeon passed low _____.

Day 08 Actions

Check UP Read and check the words you don't know.

1차 복습

- [ ] east
- [ ] west
- [ ] south
- [ ] north

- [ ] bottom
- [ ] rise
- [ ] overhead
- [ ] likely

2차 복습

- [ ] left
- [ ] right

- [ ] public
- [ ] spin

3차 복습

- [ ] wish
- [ ] engineer

- [ ] library
- [ ] professor

※ 망각 제로! 1일 전 3일 전 7일 전 학습한 단어를 복습해요.

Word Tip

east 동쪽	**west** 서쪽	**south** 남쪽	**north** 북쪽
bottom 맨 아래 (부분), 바닥	**rise** 뜨다, 오르다	**overhead** 머리 위로, 머리 위의	**likely** ~할 것 같은
left 왼쪽으로, 왼쪽의	**right** 오른쪽으로, 오른쪽의	**public** 공공의, 대중을 위한	**spin** 돌다, 회전하다
wish 바라다, 원하다	**engineer** 기술자	**library** 도서관	**professor** 교수

Rod, what happened?

Pop Quiz Choose and check the right words.

Rod knocked over and broke an action figure.

로드는 피규어를 떨어뜨려서 _____.

☐ 부수다

☐ 용서하다

Rod lied and ran out of the house.

로드는 _____ 집에서 도망쳐 나왔어요.

☐ 거짓말하다

☐ 덮다

 Listen, say, and color.

 Write the **Basic Words** and **Jump Up Words**.

break 깨다, 부수다	**The children are breaking the ice.** ⓥ 아이들이 얼음을 깨고 있어요.
kill 죽이다	**I killed the fly.** ⓥ 나는 파리를 죽였어요.
lie 거짓말하다	**I lied to my mom.** ⓥ 나는 엄마에게 거짓말했어요.

cover
덮다, 씌우다

I covered the baby with a blanket. (v)

나는 아기에게 담요를 덮어주었어요.

---

drop
떨어뜨리다, 떨어지다

He dropped a vase. (v)

그는 꽃병을 떨어뜨렸어요.

---

apology
사과

She wrote a letter of apology. (n)

그녀는 사과의 편지를 썼어요.

---

forgive
용서하다

Please forgive me. (v)

용서해 주세요.

---

happen
(일이) 일어나다, 발생하다

The car accident happened at night. (v)

그 자동차 사고는 밤에 일어났어요.

Skill UP

A Find, circle, and write the words.

1

h u b r e a k o

깨다, 부수다 _____

2

p u k i l l t h

죽이다 _____

3

c o v e r a d q

덮다, 씌우다 _____

4

d f o r g i v e

용서하다 _____

B Cross out, unscramble, and write the words.

1 (일이) 일어나다,
발생하다

p p a e n h c

_____

2 사과

p l g y a q o o

_____

3 떨어뜨리다,
떨어지다

g r d o p

_____

4 거짓말하다

e l i f

_____

60

C Connect and fill in the blanks.

1

The car accident happened at night.

그 자동차 사고는 밤에 _____.

2

She wrote a letter of apology.

그녀는 _____의 편지를 썼어요.

3

I lied to my mom.

나는 엄마에게 _____.

D Rearrange and write the sentences.

1 용서해 주세요.

| me | Please | forgive | . |

_____

_____

_____

2 그는 꽃병을 떨어뜨렸어요.

| vase | a | dropped | He | . |

_____

_____

_____

Day 09 Playtime

Check Up Read and check the words you don't know.

- [ ] break
- [ ] kill
- [ ] lie
- [ ] cover
- [ ] drop
- [ ] apology
- [ ] forgive
- [ ] happen

- [ ] voice
- [ ] present
- [ ] pregnant
- [ ] anxiety

- [ ] clear
- [ ] hurry
- [ ] ready
- [ ] passport

※ **망각 제로!** 1일 전 3일 전 7일 전 학습한 단어를 복습해요.

Word Tip

break 깨다, 부수다	**kill** 죽이다	**lie** 거짓말하다	**cover** 덮다, 씌우다
drop 떨어뜨리다, 떨어지다	**apology** 사과	**forgive** 용서하다	**happen** (일이) 일어나다, 발생하다
voice 목소리	**present** 참석한, 있는	**pregnant** 임신한	**anxiety** 불안(감)
clear 맑은, 깨끗한	**hurry** 서두르다	**ready** 준비가 된	**passport** 여권

Let's make hand shadows!

POP Quiz Choose and check the right words.

Sally and friends block the moonlight.

친구들이 달빛을 _____.

- [ ] 데려오다
- [ ] 막다

Sally makes hand shadows.

샐리는 손 _____ 를 만들어요.

- [ ] 그림자
- [ ] 염소

 **Listen & Say** Listen, say, and color.

Read & Write Write the **Basic Words** and **Jump Up Words**.

| **guess**
알아맞히다,
추측하다 | **Can you guess what's in my hand?**
내 손에 있는 게 뭔지 알아맞힐 수 있어요?

_____

_____ |

| **bring**
데려오다,
가져오다 | **Can I bring Rex to the park with us?**
렉스를 공원에 데리고 가도 될까요?

_____

_____  |

| **block**
막다,
차단하다 | **He blocked the ball.**
그는 공을 막았어요.

_____

_____  |

tonight
오늘 밤에

He will watch the animation tonight. *adv*

그는 오늘 밤에 애니메이션을 볼 거예요.

form
만들어 내다,
형태

She formed a ball out of clay. *v n*

그녀는 점토로 공을 만들었어요.

nephew
조카

He has to care for his nephew all day. *n*

그는 하루 종일 조카를 돌봐야 해요.

shadow
그림자

Children are making shadow puppets with their hands. *n*

아이들이 손으로 그림자 인형을 만들고 있어요.

goat
염소

She drew a goat. *n*

그녀는 염소를 그렸어요.

A Choose and write the words.

goat	shadow	tonight

1

_____

오늘 밤에

2

_____

그림자

3

_____

염소

B Choose and write the words.

bring	guess	nephew	block

1 알아맞히다, 추측하다

2 막다, 차단하다

3 데려오다, 가져오다

4 조카

C Connect and fill in the blanks.

1

He **blocked** the ball.

그는 공을 _____.

2

She **formed** a ball out of clay.

그녀는 점토로 공을 _____.

3

He has to care for his **nephew** all day.

그는 하루 종일 _____를 돌봐야 해요.

D Rearrange and write the sentences.

1 그녀는 염소를 그렸어요.

goat   drew   a   She   .

_____

- -

_____

_____

2 그는 오늘 밤에 애니메이션을 볼 거예요.

He   watch   tonight   will   the animation   .

_____

- -

_____

_____

Day 10 Conflicts

Read and check the words you don't know.

1차 복습

- [ ] guess
- [ ] block
- [ ] bring
- [ ] tonight
- [ ] form
- [ ] nephew
- [ ] shadow
- [ ] goat

2차 복습

- [ ] overhead
- [ ] west
- [ ] east
- [ ] likely

3차 복습

- [ ] shock
- [ ] decide
- [ ] bath
- [ ] apply

※망각 제로! 1일 전 3일 전 7일 전 학습한 단어를 복습해요.

guess 알아맞히다, 추측하다   **block** 막다, 차단하다   **bring** 데려오다, 가져오다   **tonight** 오늘 밤에
form 만들어 내다, 형태   **nephew** 조카   **shadow** 그림자   **goat** 염소
overhead 머리 위로, 머리 위의   **west** 서쪽   **east** 동쪽   **likely** ~할 것 같은
shock 충격을 주다, 충격   **decide** 결정하다   **bath** 목욕, 욕조   **apply** 바르다, 신청하다

Let's throw water bombs!

Sally and friends are playing a water bomb game.

친구들이 물 ＿＿＿＿＿＿＿ 게임을 하고 있어요.

- ☐ 폭탄
- ☐ 전투

Dennis is soaked in sweat!

데니스는 ＿＿＿＿＿＿＿ 에 흠뻑 젖었어요.

- ☐ 땀
- ☐ 걸음

Listen, say, and color.

Write the **Basic Words** and **Jump Up Words**.

bomb
폭탄, 폭격하다

There was a bomb in the building. n v

건물 안에 폭탄이 있었어요.

_____
- - - - - - - - - - -
_____

battle
전투, 싸우다

The soldier gets ready for battle. n v

그 군인은 전투 준비를 해요.

_____
- - - - - - - - - - -
_____

area
지역, 구역

We live in a bad area. n

우리는 안 좋은 지역에 살아요.

_____
- - - - - - - - - - -
_____

circle
원, 동그라미

The guards formed a circle. ⓝ

경호원들이 원을 만들었어요.

---

across
가로질러, 건너서

The soldier ran across the field. prep adv

그 군인은 들판을 가로질러 달렸어요.

---

sweat
땀

I was soaked in sweat. ⓝ

나는 땀에 흠뻑 젖었어요.

---

throw
던지다

They are throwing snowballs. ⓥ

그들은 눈덩이를 던지고 있어요.

---

step
걸음, 움직이다

He took a step back. ⓝ ⓥ

그는 뒤로 한 걸음 물러났어요.

A Choose and write the words.

bomb	area	across

①
_____
지역, 구역

②
_____
가로질러, 건너서

③
_____
폭탄, 폭격하다

B Choose and write the words.

sweat	battle	throw	step

① 던지다 _____ _____

② 땀 _____ _____

③ 전투, 싸우다 _____ _____

④ 걸음, 움직이다 _____ _____

C Unscramble and complete the sentences.

1 그 군인은 전투 준비를 해요.

t t l a e b

The soldier gets ready for _____.

2 나는 땀에 흠뻑 젖었어요.

a w e s t

I was soaked in _____.

3 경호원들이 원을 만들었어요.

c l e r c i

The guards formed a _____.

D Choose and complete the sentences.

area   bomb   across

1 우리는 안 좋은 지역에 살아요.

We live in a bad _____.

2 그 군인은 들판을 가로질러 달렸어요.

The soldier ran _____ the field.

3 건물 안에 폭탄이 있었어요.

There was a _____ in the building.

WORD PUZZLE

Complete the word puzzle.

→ Across →

① ③ ⑧

⑨ ⑩

↓ Down ↓

② ④ ⑤

⑥ ⑦

 **voice** 목소리	**present** 참석한, 있는	**restroom** 화장실	**humor** 유머, 농담	**many** 많은
speech 연설, 담화	**pregnant** 임신한	**anxiety** 불안(감)	**east** 동쪽	**west** 서쪽
south 남쪽	**north** 북쪽	**bottom** 맨 아래 (부분), 바닥	**rise** 뜨다, 오르다	**overhead** 머리 위로, 머리 위의
likely ~할 것 같은	**break** 깨다, 부수다	**kill** 죽이다	**lie** 거짓말하다	**cover** 덮다, 씌우다
drop 떨어뜨리다, 떨어지다	**apology** 사과	**forgive** 용서하다	**happen** (일이) 일어나다, 발생하다	**guess** 알아맞히다, 추측하다
bring 데려오다, 가져오다	**block** 막다, 차단하다	**tonight** 오늘 밤에	**form** 만들어 내다, 형태	**nephew** 조카
shadow 그림자	**goat** 염소	**bomb** 폭탄, 폭격하다	**battle** 전투, 싸우다	**area** 지역, 구역
circle 원, 동그라미	**across** 가로질러, 건너서	**sweat** 땀	**throw** 던지다	**step** 걸음, 움직이다

Day 06~10

#

맞힌 개수 : ☐ /40

❶ voice		㉑ 많은	
❷ present		㉒ 연설, 담화	
❸ restroom		㉓ 임신한	
❹ humor		㉔ 불안(감)	
❺ east		㉕ 맨 아래 (부분), 바닥	
❻ west		㉖ 뜨다, 오르다	
❼ south		㉗ 머리 위로, 머리 위의	
❽ north		㉘ ~할 것 같은	
❾ break		㉙ 떨어뜨리다, 떨어지다	
❿ kill		㉚ 사과	
⓫ lie		㉛ 용서하다	
⓬ happen		㉜ 덮다, 씌우다	
⓭ guess		㉝ 만들어 내다, 형태	
⓮ bring		㉞ 조카	
⓯ block		㉟ 그림자	
⓰ tonight		㊱ 염소	
⓱ bomb		㊲ 가로질러, 건너서	
⓲ battle		㊳ 땀	
⓳ area		㊴ 던지다	
⓴ circle		㊵ 걸음, 움직이다	

Part 3

FINISH

START

Day 11 Money

Check Up Read and check the words you don't know.

1차 복습

- [ ] bomb
- [ ] battle
- [ ] area
- [ ] circle
- [ ] across
- [ ] sweat
- [ ] throw
- [ ] step

2차 복습

- [ ] break
- [ ] kill
- [ ] forgive
- [ ] happen

3차 복습

- [ ] above
- [ ] hold
- [ ] now
- [ ] random

※ 망각 제로! 1일 전 3일 전 7일 전 학습한 단어를 복습해요.

Word Tip

bomb 폭탄, 폭격하다	**battle** 전투, 싸우다	**area** 지역, 구역	**circle** 원, 동그라미
across 가로질러, 건너서	**sweat** 땀	**throw** 던지다	**step** 걸음, 움직이다
break 깨다, 부수다	**kill** 죽이다	**forgive** 용서하다	**happen** (일이) 일어나다, 발생하다
above ~보다 위에	**hold** 잡고 있다, 잡다	**now** 지금, 이제	**random** 무작위의

How should I manage my money?

Pop Quiz Choose and check the right words.

Dennis has already spent all of his allowance.

데니스는 _____ 용돈을 다 썼어요.

☐ 이미, 벌써

☐ 매우

Dennis needs to manage his money.

데니스는 돈을 _____야 해요.

☐ 나누다

☐ 관리하다

 **Listen, say, and color.**

 Write the **Basic Words** and **Jump Up Words**.

pocket 주머니	**There is a hole in his pocket.** ⓝ 그의 주머니에 구멍이 하나 있어요. _____

already 이미, 벌써	**I have spent all my money already.** adv 나는 이미 돈을 다 써 버렸어요. _____

divide 나누다	**She divided up the money.** ⓥ 그녀는 돈을 나눴어요. _____

80

double
두 배의, 두 배

I had to pay double the price. (a)(n)
나는 두 배의 가격을 지불해야 했어요.

---

very
매우

It is very expensive. (adv)
그것은 매우 비싸요.

---

lack
부족, 결핍

The problem is a lack of money. (n)
문제는 자금 부족이에요.

---

manage
관리하다

You have to learn how to manage money. (v)
당신은 돈을 관리하는 법을 배워야 해요.

---

budget
예산, 비용

I have a very tight budget. (n)
나는 예산이 아주 빠듯해요.

A Find, circle, and write the words.

1

o y p o c k e t

주머니

_____

2

a l r e a d y c

이미, 벌써

_____

3

a d i v i d e k

나누다

_____

4

c l a c k o p

부족, 결핍

_____

B Cross out, unscramble, and write the words.

1 매우

e r v y u

_____

2 관리하다

g m a t n a e

_____

3 예산, 비용

r g e u d t b

_____

4 두 배의, 두배

e l c b o d u

_____

82

C Connect and fill in the blanks.

1

I had to pay double the price.

나는 _____ 가격을 지불해야 했어요.

2

I have a very tight budget.

나는 _____이 아주 빠듯해요.

3

You have to learn how to manage money.

당신은 돈을 _____ 법을 배워야 해요.

D Rearrange and write the sentences.

1 그의 주머니에 구멍이 하나 있어요.

is   There   a   his pocket   in   hole   .

_____

2 그것은 매우 비싸요.

expensive   It   very   is   .

_____

Day 12 Perception

Check Up Read and check the words you don't know.

1차 복습

- [ ] pocket
- [ ] already
- [ ] divide
- [ ] double
- [ ] very
- [ ] lack
- [ ] manage
- [ ] budget

2차 복습

- [ ] guess
- [ ] bring
- [ ] shadow
- [ ] goat

3차 복습

- [ ] restroom
- [ ] humor
- [ ] many
- [ ] speech

※망각 제로! 1일 전 3일 전 7일 전 학습한 단어를 복습해요.

Word Tip

pocket 주머니

already 이미, 벌써

divide 나누다

double 두 배의, 두 배

very 매우

lack 부족, 결핍

manage 관리하다

budget 예산, 비용

guess 알아맞히다, 추측하다

bring 데려오다, 가져오다

shadow 그림자

goat 염소

restroom 화장실

humor 유머, 농담

many 많은

speech 연설, 담화

Max, find it!

Choose and check the right words.

Some police dogs can recognize drugs by smell.

몇몇 경찰견은 _____로 마약을 인식할 수 있어요.

- [ ] 힘
- [ ] 냄새

Dennis thinks the police dog is so cool.

데니스는 경찰견이 _____ 멋지다고 생각해요.

- [ ] 정말
- [ ] ~보다

** Catch UP **

 **Listen, say, and color.**

  Write the **Basic Words** and **JUMP UP Words**.

smell 냄새, 냄새가 나다	**What a delicious smell!** n v 정말 맛있는 냄새군요! _____ - - - - - - - - - - - - - - - _____

power 힘, 능력	**He has the power to find it out.** n 그는 그것을 알아낼 힘이 있어요. _____ - - - - - - - - - - - - - - - _____

than ~보다	**Dogs smell better than humans.** prep conj 개는 사람보다 냄새를 더 잘 맡아요. _____ - - - - - - - - - - - - - - - _____

so
정말, 대단히

The dog's sense of smell is so adept. `adv`

개의 후각은 정말 뛰어나요.

behind
뒤에

A cat is standing behind him. `prep`

고양이 한 마리가 그의 뒤에 서 있어요.

visual
시각의

She has a good visual memory. `a`

그녀는 시각적인 기억력이 좋아요.

interpret
해석하다,
설명하다

They interpret the meaning of artworks. `v`

그들은 미술품의 의미를 해석해요.

recognize
알아보다,
인식하다

Dogs recognize their own scent. `v`

개들은 그들 자신의 냄새를 알아봐요.

A Choose and write the words.

behind	smell	than

1

뒤에

2

~보다

3

냄새, 냄새가 나다

B Choose and write the words.

so	visual	interpret	recognize

1 알아보다, 인식하다

2 정말, 대단히

3 해석하다, 설명하다

4 시각의

C Connect and fill in the blanks.

1. She has a good visual memory.

   그녀는 _____ 기억력이 좋아요.

2. Dogs recognize their own scent.

   개들은 그들 자신의 냄새를 _____.

3. He has the power to find it out.

   그는 그것을 알아낼 _____이 있어요.

D Rearrange and write the sentences.

1. 정말 맛있는 냄새군요!

   What   smell   delicious   a   !

   _____

   _____

   _____

2. 개는 사람보다 냄새를 더 잘 맡아요.

   better   than   Dogs   humans   smell   .

   _____

   _____

   _____

Day 13 Nature & Community

Check Up Read and check the words you don't know.

1차 복습

- [ ] smell
- [ ] power
- [ ] than
- [ ] interpret
- [ ] behind
- [ ] visual
- [ ] so
- [ ] recognize

2차 복습

- [ ] bomb
- [ ] battle
- [ ] throw
- [ ] step

3차 복습

- [ ] south
- [ ] north
- [ ] rise
- [ ] bottom

※ **망각 제로!** 1일 전 3일 전 7일 전 학습한 단어를 복습해요.

smell 냄새, 냄새가 나다
behind 뒤에
bomb 폭탄, 폭격하다
south 남쪽

power 힘, 능력
visual 시각의
battle 전투, 싸우다
north 북쪽

than ~보다
so 정말, 대단히
throw 던지다
rise 뜨다, 오르다

interpret 해석하다, 설명하다
recognize 알아보다, 인식하다
step 걸음, 움직이다
bottom 맨 아래 (부분), 바닥

90

Let's save our planet.

![Pop Quiz] **Choose and check the right words.**

We can reduce food waste.

우리는 음식물 쓰레기를 _____ 수 있어요.

☐ 금지하다

☐ 줄이다

Sally agrees with their opinions.

샐리는 친구들의 의견에 _____.

☐ 알아보다

☐ 동의하다

Read & Write Write the **Basic Words** and **Jump Up Words**.

nature 자연	**I love taking a walk in nature.** ⓝ 나는 자연에서 산책하는 것을 좋아해요. _____ _____

only 오직, 단지	**These flowers grow only in this area.** adv 이 꽃들은 오직 이 지역에서만 자라요. _____ _____

club 동아리, 클럽	**She is in the dance club.** ⓝ 그녀는 춤 동아리에 속해 있어요.  _____ _____

agree
동의하다

I agree that our community should feel safe. v

나는 우리 공동체가 안전하다고 느껴야 한다는 것에 동의해요.

---

newspaper
신문

He read about it in the newspaper. n

그는 그것을 신문에서 읽었어요.

---

reduce
줄이다

We should reduce food waste. v

우리는 음식 쓰레기를 줄여야 해요.

---

wing
날개

Birds have wings. n

새들은 날개가 있어요.

---

ban
금지하다

Smoking is banned in this building. v

이 건물에서는 흡연이 금지되어 있어요.

A Choose and write the words.

newspaper	ban	reduce

1

줄이다

2

신문

3

금지하다

B Choose and write the words.

nature	only	club	agree

1 동의하다

2 동아리, 클럽

3 자연

4 오직, 단지

C Unscramble and complete the sentences.

1 새들은 날개가 있어요.   w n g i s

Birds have _____ .

2 나는 우리 공동체가 안전하다고 느껴야   a r e g e
한다는 것에 동의해요.

I _____ that our community
should feel safe.

3 그녀는 춤 동아리에 속해 있어요.   c l b u

She is in the dance _____ .

D Choose and complete the sentences.

newspaper   nature   banned

1 나는 자연에서 산책하는 것을 좋아해요.

I love taking a walk in _____ .

2 그는 그것을 신문에서 읽었어요.

He read about it in the _____ .

3 이 건물에서는 흡연이 금지되어 있어요.

Smoking is _____ in this building.

Day 14 Leisure

Check Up Read and check the words you don't know.

1차 복습

☐ nature	☐ newspaper
☐ only	☐ reduce
☐ club	☐ wing
☐ agree	☐ ban

2차 복습

☐ pocket	☐ manage
☐ already	☐ budget

3차 복습

☐ lie	☐ drop
☐ cover	☐ apology

※ 망각 제로! 1일 전 3일 전 7일 전 학습한 단어를 복습해요.

Word Tip

nature 자연	**only** 오직, 단지	**club** 동아리, 클럽	**agree** 동의하다
newspaper 신문	**reduce** 줄이다	**wing** 날개	**ban** 금지하다
pocket 주머니	**already** 이미, 벌써	**manage** 관리하다	**budget** 예산, 비용
lie 거짓말하다	**cover** 덮다, 씌우다	**drop** 떨어뜨리다, 떨어지다	**apology** 사과

Rod had a great adventure.

PopQuiz Choose and check the right words.

Rod had a great adventure in Hawaii.

로드는 하와이에서 엄청난 _____ 을 했어요.

☐ 모험

☐ 계곡

The helicopter ride was worth the experience.

헬기 투어는 시도_____요.

☐ ~할 가치가 있는

☐ 틀림없는

Listen & Say Listen, say, and color.

Read & Write Write the Basic Words and Jump Up Words.

---

helicopter
헬리콥터

They went on a helicopter ride. ⓝ

그들은 헬리콥터 투어를 했어요.

_____

_____

_____

---

adventure
모험

He tells us about his adventures. ⓝ

그는 우리에게 그의 모험에 대해 말해줘요.

_____

_____

_____

---

aloud
큰 소리로, 크게

She read the story aloud. adv

그녀는 그 이야기를 큰 소리로 읽었어요.

_____

_____

_____

also
또한, ~도

You can also enjoy skating. `adv`

여러분은 또한 스케이트를 즐길 수 있어요.

certain
확신하는, 틀림없는

Water sports are certain to be fun. `a`

수상 스포츠는 재미있을 거라 확신해요.

worth
~할 가치가 있는

It is worth trying an extreme sport. `a`

극한스포츠를 시도해 볼 가치가 있어요.

valley
계곡, 골짜기

The valley becomes narrower at this point. `n`

이 지점에서 계곡은 좁아져요.

pleasure
즐거움, 기쁨

Amusement parks give me great pleasure. `n`

놀이공원은 나에게 큰 즐거움을 줘요.

A Find, circle, and write the words.

1. worthure

~할 가치가
있는

2. ldxaloud

큰 소리로,
크게

3. ncalsoal

또한, ~도

4. dcertain

확신하는,
틀림없는

B Cross out, unscramble, and write the words.

1. 헬리콥터   retopcheilu

2. 계곡, 골짜기   llweyav

3. 즐거움, 기쁨   aeplsoure

4. 모험   advetrnque

C Connect and fill in the blanks.

1.
They went on a helicopter ride.

그들은 _____ 투어를 했어요.

2.
He tells us about his adventures.

그는 우리에게 그의 _____에 대해 말해줘요.

3.
The valley becomes narrower at this point.

이 지점에서 _____은 좁아져요.

D Rearrange and write the sentences.

1. 그녀는 그 이야기를 큰 소리로 읽었어요.

the   story   read   aloud   She   .

_____

2. 여러분은 또한 스케이트를 즐길 수 있어요.

skating   also enjoy   You   can   .

_____

Day 15 Food Production

Check Up Read and check the words you don't know.

1차 복습

- ☐ helicopter
- ☐ adventure
- ☐ aloud
- ☐ also
- ☐ certain
- ☐ worth
- ☐ valley
- ☐ pleasure

2차 복습

- ☐ smell
- ☐ power
- ☐ interpret
- ☐ recognize

3차 복습

- ☐ block
- ☐ tonight
- ☐ form
- ☐ nephew

※ 망각 제로! 1일 전 3일 전 7일 전 학습한 단어를 복습해요.

Word Tip

helicopter 헬리콥터
certain 확신하는, 틀림없는
smell 냄새, 냄새가 나다
block 막다, 차단하다

adventure 모험
worth ~할 가치가 있는
power 힘, 능력
tonight 오늘 밤에

aloud 큰 소리로, 크게
valley 계곡, 골짜기
interpret 해석하다, 설명하다
form 만들어 내다, 형태

also 또한, ~도
pleasure 즐거움, 기쁨
recognize 알아보다, 인식하다
nephew 조카

102

We want to go to a chocolate factory.

Pop Quiz Choose and check the right words.

Dennis thinks he can eat lots of candy.

데니스는 _____ 을 많이 먹을 수 있을 거라 생각해요.

☐ 사탕
☐ 공장

The tour is offering ingredients to make chocolate.

투어에서는 초콜릿 재료를 _____.

☐ 제공하다
☐ 추가하다

 **Listen, say, and color.**

Read &Write Write the **Basic Words** and **Jump Up Words**.

factory 공장	**They gathered at the factory gates.** ⁿ 그들은 공장 정문에 모였어요. _____ ---------------------- _____

fill 채우다	**The machine fills the bottles with soda.** ^v 그 기계는 병에 탄산음료를 채워요. 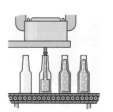 _____ ---------------------- _____

add 추가하다	**Next, add sugar to the mixture.** ^v 다음으로, 설탕을 혼합물에 추가하세요.  _____ ---------------------- _____

candy
사탕

They gave out free candy samples. *n*

그들은 샘플 사탕을 무료로 주었어요.

---

here
여기에, 여기

The chocolates are made here. *adv*

초콜릿은 여기서 만들어져요.

---

solid
단단한, 고체의

A baby can't eat solid food. *a*

아기는 단단한 음식을 먹을 수 없어요.

---

ingredient
재료, 성분

He is adding an ingredient. *n*

그는 재료를 넣고 있어요.

---

offer
제안하다,
제공하다

She offered him a job. *v*

그녀는 그에게 일자리를 제안했어요.

A Choose and write the words.

factory	fill	candy

①
_____
사탕

②
_____
채우다

③
_____
공장

B Choose and write the words.

here	solid	ingredient	offer

① 여기에, 여기
_____ _____

② 재료, 성분
_____ _____

③ 제안하다, 제공하다
_____ _____

④ 단단한, 고체의
_____ _____

C Connect and fill in the blanks.

1

Next, add sugar to the mixture.

다음으로, 설탕을 혼합물에 _____.

2

A baby can't eat solid food.

아기는 _____ 음식을 먹을 수 없어요.

3

He is adding an ingredient.

그는 _____를 넣고 있어요.

D Rearrange and write the sentences.

1 그녀는 그에게 일자리를 제안했어요.

| job | him | offered | She | a | . |

2 초콜릿은 여기서 만들어져요.

| are | The | made | here | chocolates | . |

WORD MAZE

Follow the correctly spelled words.

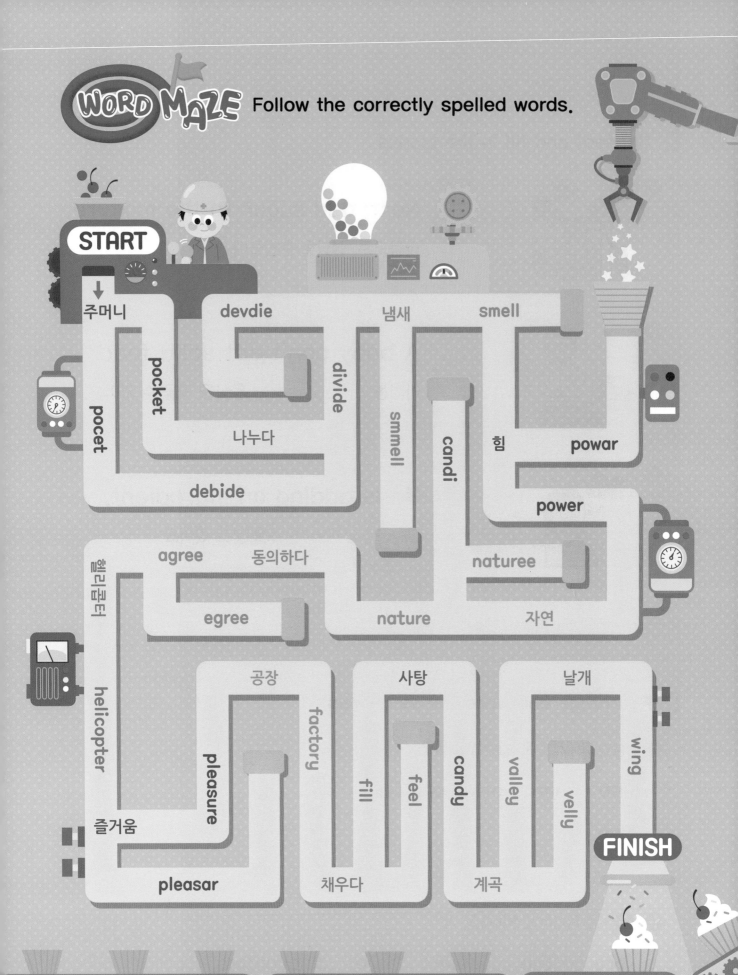

START

주머니

devdie   냄새   smell

pocket   divide

pocet   나누다   smmell   candi   힘   powar

debide   power

agree   동의하다   naturee

egree   nature   자연

헬리콥터   공장   사탕   날개

helicopter   factory   fill   feel   candy   valley   velly   wing

pleasure

즐거움   FINISH

pleasar   채우다   계곡

 **pocket** 주머니	 **already** 이미, 벌써	 **divide** 나누다	 **double** 두 배의, 두 배	**very** 매우
lack 부족, 결핍	**manage** 관리하다	**budget** 예산, 비용	**smell** 냄새, 냄새가 나다	**power** 힘, 능력
than ~보다	**so** 정말, 대단히	**behind** 뒤에	 **visual** 시각의	**interpret** 해석하다, 설명하다
recognize 알아보다, 인식하다	**nature** 자연	**only** 오직, 단지	 **club** 동아리, 클럽	**agree** 동의하다
newspaper 신문	**reduce** 줄이다	**wing** 날개	 **ban** 금지하다	**helicopter** 헬리콥터
adventure 모험	**aloud** 큰 소리로, 크게	**also** 또한, ~도	 **certain** 확신하는, 틀림없는	**worth** ~할 가치가 있는
valley 계곡, 골짜기	**pleasure** 즐거움, 기쁨	**factory** 공장	**fill** 채우다	**add** 추가하다
candy 사탕	 **here** 여기에, 여기	 **solid** 단단한, 고체의	 **ingredient** 재료, 성분	**offer** 제안하다, 제공하다

Day 11~15

#

맞힌 개수 : ☐ / 40

① pocket		㉑ 매우	
② already		㉒ 부족, 결핍	
③ manage		㉓ 나누다	
④ double		㉔ 예산, 비용	
⑤ smell		㉕ 뒤에	
⑥ power		㉖ 시각의	
⑦ than		㉗ 해석하다, 설명하다	
⑧ so		㉘ 알아보다, 인식하다	
⑨ nature		㉙ 신문	
⑩ only		㉚ 줄이다	
⑪ club		㉛ 날개	
⑫ agree		㉜ 금지하다	
⑬ certain		㉝ 헬리콥터	
⑭ adventure		㉞ ~할 가치가 있는	
⑮ aloud		㉟ 계곡, 골짜기	
⑯ also		㊱ 즐거움, 기쁨	
⑰ factory		㊲ 여기에, 여기	
⑱ fill		㊳ 단단한, 고체의	
⑲ add		㊴ 재료, 성분	
⑳ offer		㊵ 사탕	

Part 4

FINISH

START

Day 16 Competition

Check Up Read and check the words you don't know.

1차 복습

- [ ] factory
- [ ] fill
- [ ] add
- [ ] candy
- [ ] here
- [ ] solid
- [ ] ingredient
- [ ] offer

2차 복습

- [ ] nature
- [ ] only
- [ ] wing
- [ ] ban

3차 복습

- [ ] area
- [ ] circle
- [ ] across
- [ ] sweat

※ 망각 제로! 1일 전 3일 전 7일 전 학습한 단어를 복습해요.

factory 공장	**fill** 채우다	**add** 추가하다	**candy** 사탕
here 여기에, 여기	**solid** 단단한, 고체의	**ingredient** 재료, 성분	**offer** 제안하다, 제공하다
nature 자연	**only** 오직, 단지	**wing** 날개	**ban** 금지하다
area 지역, 구역	**circle** 원, 동그라미	**across** 가로질러, 건너서	**sweat** 땀

We hope Sally wins the contest.

POP Quiz Choose and check the right words.

There's a writing contest.

글짓기 _____ 가 있어요.

- [ ] 대회
- [ ] 상품

Sally passed the preliminary round.

샐리는 예선을 _____.

- [ ] 통과하다
- [ ] 이기다

Listen & Say Listen, say, and color.

Read & Write Write the **Basic Words** and **Jump Up Words**.

| **win** 이기다, (이겨서 무엇을) 따다 | **She hopes to win the gold medal.** ⓥ
그녀는 금메달 따기를 희망해요.
_____
_____ |

| **prize** 상, 상품 | **I won first prize in the contest.** ⓝ
나는 그 대회에서 1등 상을 받았어요.
_____
_____ |

| **contest** 대회, 시합, 경쟁을 벌이다 | **The contest will take place in Seoul.** ⓝ ⓥ
그 대회는 서울에서 열릴 거예요.
_____
_____ |

pass
지나가다, 통과하다

They clapped as the runners passed. v

그들은 주자들이 지나갈 때 박수를 쳤어요.

gold
금, 금빛의

How does it feel to win a gold medal? n a

금메달을 딴 기분이 어때요?

final
결승전, 마지막의

He can take part in the final. n a

그는 결승전에 참가할 수 있어요.

round
(대회에서)
라운드, 회

I moved on to the next round. n

나는 다음 라운드에 진출했어요.

glory
영광, 영예

She enjoyed her moment of glory. n

그녀는 영광의 순간을 즐겼어요.

A Choose and write the words.

win	prize	contest

1

_____
_____
_____

대회, 시합,
경쟁을 벌이다

2

_____
_____
_____

이기다,
(이겨서 무엇을) 따다

3

_____
_____
_____

상, 상품

B Choose and write the words.

pass	gold	round	glory

1 지나다가, 통과하다

2 (대회에서) 라운드, 회

3 영광, 영예

4 금, 금빛의

C Unscramble and complete the sentences.

1 금메달을 딴 기분이 어때요?   o d g l

How does it feel to win a _____
medal?

2 그녀는 영광의 순간을 즐겼어요.   g l y o r

She enjoyed her moment of

_____ .

3 그들은 주자들이 지나갈 때 박수를 쳤어요.   e d a p s s

They clapped as the runners

_____ .

D Choose and complete the sentences.

contest   final   prize

1 나는 그 대회에서 1등 상을 받았어요.

I won first _____ in the contest.

2 그는 결승전에 참가할 수 있어요.

He can take part in the _____ .

3 그 대회는 서울에서 열릴 거예요.

The _____ will take place in Seoul.

117

Day 17 Religion

Check UP Read and check the words you don't know.

1차 복습

- [ ] prize
- [ ] glory
- [ ] pass
- [ ] contest
- [ ] gold
- [ ] final
- [ ] round
- [ ] win

2차 복습

- [ ] adventure
- [ ] valley
- [ ] helicopter
- [ ] pleasure

3차 복습

- [ ] divide
- [ ] very
- [ ] double
- [ ] lack

※ 망각 제로! 1일 전 3일 전 7일 전 학습한 단어를 복습해요.

 Word Tip

prize 상, 상품 glory 영광, 영예 pass 지나가다, 통과하다 contest 대회, 시합, 경쟁을 벌이다
gold 금, 금빛의 final 결승전, 마지막의 round (대회에서) 라운드, 회 win 이기다, (이겨서 무엇을) 따다
adventure 모험 valley 계곡, 골짜기 helicopter 헬리콥터 pleasure 즐거움, 기쁨
divide 나누다 very 매우 double 두 배의, 두 배 lack 부족, 결핍

What is heaven like?

![Pop Quiz] **Choose and check the right words.**

Rod wonders if Kiara believes in God.

로드는 키아라가 _____ 을 믿는지 궁금해요.

☐ 종교
☐ 신

Kiara hopes there is a heaven.

키아라는 _____ 이 있길 바라요.

☐ 천국
☐ 지옥

Read & Write Write the **Basic Words** and **Jump Up Words**.

heaven 천국, 하늘나라	**Imagine what heaven would be like.** [n] 천국이 어떨지 상상해 보세요. _____ _____ _____

god 신	**Do you believe in God?** [n] 당신은 신을 믿나요? _____ _____ _____

dead 죽은 사람들, 죽은	**They said a prayer for the dead.** [n] [a] 그들은 돌아가신 분들을 위한 기도를 했어요. _____ _____ _____

way
방식, 방법

This is the way we mourn our loss. (n)

이것이 우리의 상실을 애도하는 방식이에요.

---

during
~ 동안

They honored his life during his funeral. (prep)

그들은 그의 장례식 동안 그의 삶을 기렸어요.

---

hell
지옥

The prison was like hell on earth. (n)

그 감옥은 지옥 같았어요.

---

religion
종교

My parents' religion is important to them. (n)

부모님의 종교는 그들에게 중요해요.

---

exist
존재하다

Do you think God exists? (v)

당신은 신이 존재한다고 생각하나요?

A Find, circle, and write the words.

1

o c e x i s t r

존재하다

_____

2

r e l i g i o n i

종교

_____

3

h e l l a r z i

지옥

_____

4

d u r i n g f n

~ 동안

_____

B Cross out, unscramble, and write the words.

1 죽은 사람들, 죽은

g a e d d

_____

2 방식, 방법

y a w p

_____

3 천국, 하늘나라

n v a e e h q

_____

4 신

g d z o

_____

C Connect and fill in the blanks.

1

Do you believe in God?

당신은 _____을 믿나요?

2

This is the way we mourn our loss.

이것이 우리의 상실을 애도하는 _____이에요.

3

Imagine what heaven would be like.

_____이 어떨지 상상해 보세요.

D Rearrange and write the sentences.

1 당신은 신이 존재한다고 생각하나요?

Do   think   you   exists   God   ?

_____
- -
_____

2 그들은 돌아가신 분들을 위한 기도를 했어요.

a prayer   said   for   They   the   dead   .

_____
- -
_____

Day 18 Communication

Check Up Read and check the words you don't know.

1차 복습

☐ heaven	☐ during
☐ god	☐ hell
☐ dead	☐ religion
☐ way	☐ exist

2차 복습

☐ factory	☐ ingredient
☐ fill	☐ offer

3차 복습

☐ than	☐ behind
☐ so	☐ visual

※ 망각 제로! 1일 전 3일 전 7일 전 학습한 단어를 복습해요.

Word Tip

heaven 천국, 하늘나라	**god** 신	**dead** 죽은 사람들, 죽은	**way** 방식, 방법
during ~동안	**hell** 지옥	**religion** 종교	**exist** 존재하다
factory 공장	**fill** 채우다	**ingredient** 재료, 성분	**offer** 제안하다, 제공하다
than ~보다	**so** 정말, 대단히	**behind** 뒤에	**visual** 시각의

How do I send a letter by mail?

Pop Quiz Choose and check the right words.

How do I send mail?

어떻게 _____을 보내나요?

| 우편 |
| 사무소 |

Maybe Dennis's letters will be returned.

아마 데니스의 편지는 _____ 거예요.

| 돌아오다 |
| 접다 |

125

 **Listen, say, and color.**

Read & Write **Write the Basic Words and Jump Up Words.**

mail 우편, (우편으로) 보내다	The magazine will be sent by mail. ⓝ ⓥ 잡지는 우편으로 보내드려요.

return 돌아오다, 돌아가다	She has returned from overseas. ⓥ 그녀는 해외에서 돌아왔어요.

own 자신의, 소유하다	Animals use their own language. ⓐ ⓥ 동물들은 그들 자신만의 언어를 사용해요.

126

office
사무실, 사무소

I will stay late at the office tonight. *n*

나는 오늘 밤늦게까지 사무실에 있을 거예요.

---

inside
~의 안에, 안으로

There's a letter inside the mailbox. *prep* *adv*

그 우편함 안에는 편지가 있어요.

---

envelope
봉투

He writes her address on the envelope. *n*

그는 봉투에 그녀의 주소를 써요.

---

fold
접다

She folded the paper in half. *v*

그녀는 종이를 반으로 접었어요.

---

without
~ 없이

They need to communicate without fighting. *prep*

그들은 싸우지 않고 의사소통할 필요가 있어요.

A Choose and write the words.

mail   return   inside

1

421 Homelearn-ro
Iscream-gu,
Seoul,
Republic of Korea
00000

16 Digital-ro, Nam-gu,
Gwangju,
Republic of Korea

2

3

우편, (우편으로) 보내다   ~의 안에, 안으로   돌아오다, 돌아가다

B Choose and write the words.

office   own   envelope   without

1 봉투

2 사무실, 사무소

3 자신의, 소유하다

4 ~ 없이

C Connect and fill in the blanks.

1.

He writes her address on the envelope.

그는 _____에 그녀의 주소를 써요.

2.

She folded the paper in half.

그녀는 종이를 반으로 _____.

3.

I will stay late at the office tonight.

나는 오늘 밤늦게까지 _____에 있을 거예요.

D Rearrange and write the sentences.

1 잡지는 우편으로 보내드려요.

magazine   The   by mail   be   will   sent   .

_____

2 그녀는 해외에서 돌아왔어요.

from   She   overseas   has   returned   .

_____

Day 19 Social Interaction

Check Up Read and check the words you don't know.

1차 복습

- ☐ mail
- ☐ return
- ☐ own
- ☐ office

- ☐ inside
- ☐ envelope
- ☐ fold
- ☐ without

2차 복습

- ☐ win
- ☐ prize

- ☐ round
- ☐ glory

3차 복습

- ☐ club
- ☐ agree

- ☐ newspaper
- ☐ reduce

※ 망각 제로! 1일 전 3일 전 7일 전 학습한 단어를 복습해요.

Word Tip

mail 우편, (우편으로) 보내다
inside ~의 안에, 안으로
win 이기다, (이겨서 무엇을) 따다
club 동아리, 클럽

return 돌아오다, 돌아가다
envelope 봉투
prize 상, 상품
agree 동의하다

own 자신의, 소유하다
fold 접다
round (대회에서) 라운드, 회
newspaper 신문

office 사무실, 사무소
without ~ 없이
glory 영광, 영예
reduce 줄이다

130

A new smartphone is out!

Mong watched the video introducing the new smartphone.

몽은 새로운 휴대폰을 _____ 영상을 봤어요.

☐	소개하다
☐	소통하다

You can chat with your phone.

휴대폰과 _____ 수 있어요.

☐	수다를 떨다
☐	줄이다

Listen & Say Listen, say, and color.

Read & Write Write the **Basic Words** and **Jump Up Words**.

forever 영원히	**adv** **Our friendship will last forever.** 우리의 우정은 영원할 거예요. _____ _____

company 회사	**n** **He retired from the company last year.** 그는 작년에 회사에서 퇴직하셨어요. _____ _____

introduce 소개하다, 도입하다	**v** **They want to introduce the new technology.** 그들은 그 새로운 기술을 소개하고 싶어 해요. _____ _____

however
하지만, 그러나

However, he is shy. *adv*

하지만, 그는 수줍음이 많아요.

_____
- - - - - - - - - - - - - - - - - - - -
_____

gesture
몸짓

We used gestures to communicate. *n*

우리는 몸짓으로 의사소통을 했어요.

_____
- - - - - - - - - - - - - - - - - - - -
_____

interact
소통하다

They can interact with each other. *v*

그들은 서로 소통할 수 있어요.

_____
- - - - - - - - - - - - - - - - - - - -
_____

pattern
양식, 패턴

They are changing patterns of behavior. *n*

그들은 행동 양식을 바꾸고 있어요.

_____
- - - - - - - - - - - - - - - - - - - -
_____

chat
수다를 떨다, 대화하다

The two friends chatted all evening. *v*

두 친구는 저녁 내내 수다를 떨었어요.

_____
- - - - - - - - - - - - - - - - - - - -
_____

A Choose and write the words.

gesture	pattern	interact

1

_____

_____

_____

소통하다

2

_____

_____

_____

양식, 패턴

3

_____

_____

_____

몸짓

B Choose and write the words.

however	forever	introduce	company

1 영원히

2 소개하다, 도입하다

3 하지만, 그러나

4 회사

C Unscramble and complete the sentences.

1 우리의 우정은 영원할 거예요.

e e v f r o r

Our friendship will last _____ .

2 그는 작년에 회사에서 퇴직하셨어요.

p a c m o n y

He retired from the _____ last year.

3 두 친구는 저녁 내내 수다를 떨었어요.

a h t c t e d

The two friends _____ all evening.

D Choose and complete the sentences.

patterns   interact   introduce

1 그들은 서로 소통할 수 있어요.

They can _____ with each other.

2 그들은 행동 양식을 바꾸고 있어요.

They are changing _____ of behavior.

3 그들은 그 새로운 기술을 소개하고 싶어 해요.

They want to _____ the new technology.

Day 20 Social Issues

Check Up — Read and check the words you don't know.

1차 복습

☐ forever	☐ gesture
☐ company	☐ interact
☐ introduce	☐ pattern
☐ however	☐ chat

2차 복습

☐ heaven	☐ religion
☐ god	☐ exist

3차 복습

☐ aloud	☐ certain
☐ also	☐ worth

※ 망각 제로! 1일 전 3일 전 7일 전 학습한 단어를 복습해요.

Word Tip

forever 영원히	**company** 회사	**introduce** 소개하다, 도입하다	**however** 하지만, 그러나
gesture 몸짓	**interact** 소통하다	**pattern** 양식, 패턴	**chat** 수다를 떨다, 대화하다
heaven 천국, 하늘나라	**god** 신	**religion** 종교	**exist** 존재하다
aloud 큰 소리로, 크게	**also** 또한, ~도	**certain** 확신하는, 틀림없는	**worth** ~할 가치가 있는

Let's discuss the pros and cons of zoos.

토론 수업 시간이에요.

동물원에 대해 찬반 토론을 해 보아요.
Let's discuss the pros and cons of zoos.
먼저, 찬성하는 쪽 의견을 들어 볼까요?

우리는 동물원에서 많은 동물들을 볼 수 있어요.

멸종 위기 동물을 보호할 수도 있어요.

그럼 반대 의견도 들어 볼까요?

동물원에 갇혀 지내는 건 야생 동물에게 너무 가혹해요.
It's too harsh for animals to be stuck in cages.

동물들은 인형이 아니에요.
Animals are not dolls.

Pop Quiz Choose and check the right words.

It's too harsh for animals to be stuck in cages.

동물이 우리에 갇혀 지내는 것은 ＿＿＿＿＿요.

[ ] 확신하는
[ ] 가혹한

Dennis said, "Animals are not dolls."

데니스는 "동물은 ＿＿＿＿＿이 아니야."라고 말했어요.

[ ] 인형
[ ] 우리

Catch Up

Read & Write Write the **Basic Words** and **Jump Up Words**.

discuss 논의하다	**We discussed closing the zoo.** ^v 우리는 동물원 폐쇄에 대해 논의했어요.

kid 아이	**The kids want to go to the zoo.** ⁿ 아이들이 동물원에 가고 싶어 해요.

cage 우리, 새장	**A monkey is dancing in the cage.** ⁿ 원숭이 한 마리가 우리 안에서 춤추고 있어요.

138

wood
숲, 나무

Woods **are home to wildlife.** ⓝ
숲은 야생 동물의 서식지예요.

doll
인형

Do you have dolls **of different races?** ⓝ
다양한 인종의 인형이 있나요?

sacrifice
희생하다, 희생

She sacrificed **everything for her children.** ⓥ ⓝ
그녀는 자녀들을 위해 모든 것을 희생했어요.

disagree
동의하지 않다

I disagree **with their opinion.** ⓥ
나는 그들의 의견에 동의하지 않아요.

harsh
가혹한, 혹독한

That's too harsh **of a punishment.** ⓐ
그것은 너무 가혹한 처벌이에요.

A Find, circle, and write the words.

1
d i s c u s s r l

논의하다

2
s a c r i f i c e

희생하다,
희생

3
h c a g e i k e

우리, 새장

4
v p a d o l l t

인형

B Cross out, unscramble, and write the words

1 아이
k i p d

2 가혹한, 혹독한
h r h a s e

3 동의하지 않다
e h e a s d i g r

4 숲, 나무
d o w o v

C Connect and fill in the blanks.

①

I **disagree** with their opinion.

나는 그들의 의견에 _____.

②

Woods are home to wildlife.

_____은 야생 동물의 서식지예요.

③

The kids **want to go** to the zoo.

_____들이 동물원에 가고 싶어 해요.

D Rearrange and write the sentences.

① 원숭이 한 마리가 우리 안에서 춤추고 있어요.

is   in   the cage   A monkey   dancing   .

_____

_____

_____

② 우리는 동물원 폐쇄에 대해 논의했어요.

discussed   We   closing   zoo   the   .

_____

_____

_____

WORD PUZZLE Complete the word puzzle.

ACROSS

③ The two friends _____ted all evening.

④ Do you believe in _____?

⑦ I won first _____ in the contest.

⑨ _____, he is shy.

⑩ Do you have _____s of different races?

DOWN

① This is the _____ we mourn our loss.

② The _____s want to go to the zoo.

⑤ She hopes to _____ the gold medal.

⑥ She has _____ed from overseas.

⑧ She _____ed the paper in half.

Day 16~20

win 이기다, (이겨서 무엇을) 따다	**prize** 상, 상품	**contest** 대회, 시합, 경쟁을 벌이다	**pass** 지나가다, 통과하다	**gold** 금, 금빛의
final 결승전, 마지막의	**round** (대회에서) 라운드, 회	**glory** 영광, 영예	**heaven** 천국, 하늘나라	**god** 신
dead 죽은 사람들, 죽은	**way** 방식, 방법	**during** ~ 동안	**hell** 지옥	**religion** 종교
exist 존재하다	**mail** 우편, (우편으로) 보내다	**return** 돌아오다, 돌아가다	**own** 자신의, 소유하다	**office** 사무실, 사무소
inside ~의 안에, 안으로	**envelope** 봉투	**fold** 접다	**without** ~ 없이	**forever** 영원히
company 회사	**introduce** 소개하다, 도입하다	**however** 하지만, 그러나	**gesture** 몸짓	**interact** 소통하다
pattern 양식, 패턴	**chat** 수다를 떨다, 대화하다	**discuss** 논의하다	**kid** 아이	**cage** 우리, 새장
wood 숲, 나무	**doll** 인형	**sacrifice** 희생하다, 희생	**disagree** 동의하지 않다	**harsh** 가혹한, 혹독한

맞힌 개수 : ☐ / 40

❶ win		㉑ 금, 금빛의	
❷ round		㉒ 결승전, 마지막의	
❸ contest		㉓ 상, 상품	
❹ pass		㉔ 영광, 영예	
❺ heaven		㉕ ~ 동안	
❻ god		㉖ 지옥	
❼ dead		㉗ 종교	
❽ way		㉘ 존재하다	
❾ mail		㉙ ~의 안에, 안으로	
❿ return		㉚ 봉투	
⓫ own		㉛ 접다	
⓬ office		㉜ ~ 없이	
⓭ forever		㉝ 몸짓	
⓮ company		㉞ 소통하다	
⓯ introduce		㉟ 양식, 패턴	
⓰ chat		㊱ 하지만, 그러나	
⓱ discuss		㊲ 인형	
⓲ kid		㊳ 희생하다, 희생	
⓳ cage		㊴ 동의하지 않다	
⓴ wood		㊵ 가혹한, 혹독한	

Part 5

FINISH

START

Day 21 Exhibitions & Performances

1차 복습

- [ ] discuss
- [ ] kid
- [ ] cage
- [ ] wood
- [ ] doll
- [ ] sacrifice
- [ ] disagree
- [ ] harsh

2차 복습

- [ ] mail
- [ ] return
- [ ] fold
- [ ] without

3차 복습

- [ ] add
- [ ] candy
- [ ] here
- [ ] solid

※ 망각 제로! 1일 전 3일 전 7일 전 학습한 단어를 복습해요.

Word Tip

discuss 논의하다	kid 아이	cage 우리, 새장	wood 숲, 나무
doll 인형	sacrifice 희생하다, 희생	disagree 동의하지 않다	harsh 가혹한, 혹독한
mail 우편, (우편으로) 보내다	return 돌아오다, 돌아가다	fold 접다	without ~ 없이
add 추가하다	candy 사탕	here 여기에, 여기	solid 단단한, 고체의

We're in the Natural History Museum.

PoP Quiz Choose and check the right words.

A giant bone is hanging from the ceiling.

_____ 뼈 하나가 천장에 걸려 있어요.

☐ 거대한

☐ 초등의

A woman is explaining an exhibit.

한 여성분이 _____ 을 설명해줘요.

☐ 전시품

☐ 박물관

Catch Up

 **Listen & Say** Listen, say, and color.

Read & Write Write the **Basic Words** and **Jump Up Words**.

museum 박물관	**They visited the local museum.** ⓝ 그들은 지역 박물관을 방문했어요. _____ _____

elementary 초등의, 초급의	**Elementary students go on a field trip.** ⓐ 초등학생들이 현장 학습을 가요. _____ _____

giant 거대한, 거인	**There was a giant dinosaur skeleton.** ⓐⓝ 거대한 공룡 뼈가 있었어요. _____ _____

point
핵심, 요점,
가리키다

The point of the costume is to make people laugh. n v

그 의상의 핵심은 사람들을 웃게 만드는 것이에요.

---

hang
걸다, 매달다

The dinosaur skeleton was hung from the ceiling. v

그 공룡 뼈는 천장에 걸려 있었어요.

---

exhibit
전시하다, 전시품

The crown was first exhibited there. v n

그 왕관은 그곳에서 처음 전시되었어요.

---

explain
설명하다

The magician explained his magic trick. v

마술사는 그의 마술 묘기를 설명했어요.

---

absorb
흡수하다,
받아들이다

Children absorb everything around them. v

아이들은 주변의 모든 것을 흡수해요.

A Choose and write the words.

museum	elementary	giant

1

_____
- - - - - - - - - - - -
_____

거대한, 거인

2

_____
- - - - - - - - - - - -
_____

초등의, 초급의

3

_____
- - - - - - - - - - - -
_____

박물관

B Choose and write the words.

point	hang	exhibit	explain

1 걸다, 매달다

2 핵심, 요점, 가리키다

3 설명하다

4 전시하다, 전시품

C Connect and fill in the blanks.

① **Children absorb everything around them.**

아이들은 주변의 모든 것을 ＿＿＿＿＿＿＿＿.

② **The crown was first exhibited there.**

그 왕관은 그곳에서 처음 ＿＿＿＿＿＿＿＿.

③ **The magician explained his magic trick.**

마술사는 그의 마술 묘기를 ＿＿＿＿＿＿＿＿.

D Rearrange and write the sentences.

① 그들은 지역 박물관을 방문했어요.

| museum | They | local | visited | the | . |

＿＿＿＿＿＿＿＿＿＿＿＿＿＿＿＿＿＿＿＿＿＿＿＿

② 초등학생들이 현장 학습을 가요.

| go | on | Elementary | a field trip | students | . |

＿＿＿＿＿＿＿＿＿＿＿＿＿＿＿＿＿＿＿＿＿＿＿＿

Day 22 Clothing

Check Up Read and check the words you don't know.

1차 복습

☐ museum   ☐ hang
☐ elementary   ☐ exhibit
☐ giant   ☐ explain
☐ point   ☐ absorb

2차 복습

☐ forever   ☐ pattern
☐ company   ☐ chat

3차 복습

☐ gold   ☐ final
☐ pass   ☐ contest

※ 망각 제로! 1일 전 3일 전 7일 전 학습한 단어를 복습해요.

Word Tip

museum 박물관	**elementary** 초등의, 초급의	**giant** 거대한, 거인	**point** 핵심, 요점, 가리키다
hang 걸다, 매달다	**exhibit** 전시하다, 전시품	**explain** 설명하다	**absorb** 흡수하다, 받아들이다
forever 영원히	**company** 회사	**pattern** 양식, 패턴	**chat** 수다를 떨다, 대화하다
gold 금, 금빛의	**pass** 지나가다, 통과하다	**final** 결승전, 마지막의	**contest** 대회, 시합, 경쟁을 벌이다

Sally got cotton flowers as a gift.

POP Quiz Choose and check the right words.

Do you know that your shirt is made of cotton?

셔츠는 _____ 로 만들어진 거 알고 있니?

- [ ] 목화
- [ ] 금

Kiara's jeans must be made of cotton.

키아라의 _____ 는 목화로 만들어진 것이 틀림없어요.

- [ ] 왕관
- [ ] 청바지

153

Listen & Say Listen, say, and color.

Read & Write Write the **Basic Words** and **Jump Up Words**.

cotton 면, 목화	**This shirt is made of cotton.** 이 셔츠는 면으로 만들어졌어요.

clothes 옷, 의복	**These clothes are in fashion.** 이 옷들이 유행이에요.

jeans 청바지	**These jeans have many pockets.** 이 청바지에는 주머니가 많아요.

from ~으로 (만들어진), ~부터	**Is this shirt made from pure cotton?** `prep` 이 셔츠는 순면으로 만들어졌나요?

crown 왕관	**She wore a crown with many jewels.** `n` 그녀는 많은 보석이 박힌 왕관을 썼어요.

fabric 천, 직물	**This fabric comes in many colors.** `n` 이 천은 여러 가지 색상이 있어요.

wool 모직, 울	**This coat is 100% wool.** `n` 이 코트는 100% 모직이에요.

lamb 어린 양	**Lamb's wool is warm and cozy.** `n` 양털은 따뜻하고 포근해요.

A Choose and write the words.

cotton	jeans	crown

①

면, 목화

②

왕관

③

청바지

B Choose and write the words.

from	lamb	wool	fabric

① 천, 직물

② 모직, 울

③ 어린 양

④ ~으로 (만들어진), ~부터

C Unscramble and complete the sentences.

1 양털은 따뜻하고 포근해요. `m a L b`

_____'s wool is warm and cozy.

2 이 코트는 100% 모직이에요. `w l o o`

This coat is 100% _____.

3 이 옷들이 유행이에요. `l o c e s t h`

These _____ are in fashion.

D Choose and complete the sentences.

cotton   fabric   jeans

1 이 천은 여러 가지 색상이 있어요.

This _____ comes in many colors.

2 이 청바지에는 주머니가 많아요.

These _____ have many pockets.

3 이 셔츠는 면으로 만들어졌어요.

This shirt is made of _____.

Day 23 Performance

Check Up Read and check the words you don't know.

1차 복습

- [ ] cotton
- [ ] clothes
- [ ] jeans
- [ ] from
- [ ] crown
- [ ] fabric
- [ ] wool
- [ ] lamb

2차 복습

- [ ] discuss
- [ ] kid
- [ ] disagree
- [ ] harsh

3차 복습

- [ ] dead
- [ ] way
- [ ] during
- [ ] hell

※ 망각 제로! 1일 전 3일 전 7일 전 학습한 단어를 복습해요.

Word Tip

cotton 면, 목화

crown 왕관

discuss 논의하다

dead 죽은 사람들, 죽은

clothes 옷, 의복

fabric 천, 직물

kid 아이

way 방식, 방법

jeans 청바지

wool 모직, 울

disagree 동의하지 않다

during ~ 동안

from ~으로 (만들어진), ~부터

lamb 어린 양

harsh 가혹한, 혹독한

hell 지옥

Let's decide the roles of the play!

POP Quiz Choose and check the right words.

Sally will play a gentleman.

샐리는 _____를 연기할 거예요.

Kiara will play a lady.

키아라는 _____을 연기할 거예요.

☐ 커플

☐ 신사, 양반

☐ 장면

☐ 여성, 숙녀

159

 **Listen & Say** Listen, say, and color.

Read & Write Write the **Basic Words** and **Jump Up Words**.

act 연기하다, 행동하다	**He is** acting **as an elegant lady.** ⓥ 그는 우아한 숙녀 연기를 하고 있어요.

lady 여성, 숙녀	**Please show this** lady **to her seat.** ⓝ 이 여성을 자리로 안내해 주세요.

gentleman 신사, 양반	**He introduced the** gentleman **to me.** ⓝ 그는 나에게 그 신사를 소개했어요.

160

fool
바보, 어릿광대

He played a fool in the play. (n)

그는 연극에서 바보 역할을 했어요.

_____

- -

_____

couple
커플, 두 사람

The couple plans to dance on the stage. (n)

그 커플은 무대에서 춤을 출 계획이에요.

_____

- -

_____

beard
(턱)수염

She wore a fake beard for her role. (n)

그녀는 자신의 역할을 위해 가짜 수염을 썼어요.

_____

- -

_____

scene
장면, 현장

The last scene was impressive. (n)

마지막 장면이 인상적이었어요.

_____

- -

_____

recall
생각나게 하다,
기억해 내다

I could recall the main actor's name. (v)

나는 주연 배우의 이름이 생각났어요.

_____

- -

_____

A Choose and write the words.

act	lady	couple

1

여성, 숙녀

2

커플, 두 사람

3

연기하다, 행동하다

B Choose and write the words.

gentleman	fool	beard	scene

1 바보, 어릿광대

2 장면, 현장

3 신사, 양반

4 (턱)수염

C Connect and fill in the blanks.

1

She wore a fake beard for her role.

그녀는 자신의 역할을 위해 가짜 _____을 썼어요.

2

He played a fool in the play.

그는 연극에서 _____ 역할을 했어요.

3

He introduced the gentleman to me.

그는 나에게 그 _____를 소개했어요.

D Rearrange and write the sentences.

1 그는 우아한 숙녀 연기를 하고 있어요.

is   He   acting   as   an   elegant lady   .

_____

- -

_____

2 나는 주연 배우의 이름이 생각났어요.

main actor's   name   recall   I   the   could   .

_____

- -

_____

Check Up Read and check the words you don't know.

1차 복습

- [ ] act
- [ ] couple
- [ ] lady
- [ ] beard
- [ ] gentleman
- [ ] scene
- [ ] fool
- [ ] recall

2차 복습

- [ ] museum
- [ ] elementary
- [ ] explain
- [ ] absorb

3차 복습

- [ ] own
- [ ] envelope
- [ ] office
- [ ] inside

※망각 제로! 1일 전 3일 전 7일 전 학습한 단어를 복습해요.

Word Tip

act 연기하다, 행동하다	lady 여성, 숙녀	gentleman 신사, 양반	fool 바보, 어릿광대
couple 커플, 두 사람	beard (턱)수염	scene 장면, 현장	recall 기억해 내다, 생각나게 하다
museum 박물관	explain 설명하다	elementary 초등의, 초급의	absorb 흡수하다, 받아들이다
own 자신의, 소유하다	office 사무실, 사무소	envelope 봉투	inside ~의 안에, 안으로

What is the 5W1H method?

POP Quiz Choose and check the right words.

Sally suggests using the 5W1H method
to write an article.

샐리는 육하원칙 _____ 을 사용해서 기사를 쓸 것을 제안해요.

☐ 방법

☐ 장면

Kiara can write a clear situation **with**
the 5W1H method.

키아라는 육하원칙 방법으로 명확한 _____ 을 쓸 수 있어요.

☐ 언제

☐ 상황

 Write the Basic Words and Jump Up Words.

---

who
누구

pron

Who opened the door?

누가 문을 열었나요?

_____
- -
_____

---

when
언제

adv **pron**

When did you last see her?

그녀를 언제 마지막으로 보았죠?

_____
- -
_____

---

where
어디에

adv

Where do you live?

당신은 어디에 사세요?

_____
- -
_____

how
어떻게

How can I use it?

그것을 어떻게 사용하나요?

adv

---

why
왜

Why were you busy?

당신은 왜 바빴나요?

adv

---

situation
상황

He explained the situation to them.

그는 그들에게 상황을 설명했어요.

n

---

method
방법

You can choose a new method.

당신은 새로운 방법을 선택할 수 있어요.

n

---

obvious
명백한, 분명한

The answer to this problem is obvious.

이 문제에 대한 답은 명백해요.

a

A Choose and write the words.

who	when	where

① 언제

② 어디에

③ 누구

B Choose and write the words.

how	why	situation	method

① 어떻게

② 상황

③ 왜

④ 방법

C Unscramble and complete the sentences.

1 이 문제에 대한 답은 명백해요.   o b i s u v o

The answer to this problem is

_____.

2 그것을 어떻게 사용하나요?   w o H

_____ can I use it?

3 당신은 왜 바빴나요?   h y W

_____ were you busy?

D Choose and complete the sentences.

When   Where   situation

1 그는 그들에게 상황을 설명했어요.

He explained the _____ to them.

2 그녀를 언제 마지막으로 보았죠?

_____ did you last see her?

3 당신은 어디에 사세요?

_____ do you live?

Day 25 Science & Products

Check Up Read and check the words you don't know.

1차 복습

- [ ] who
- [ ] when
- [ ] where
- [ ] how
- [ ] why
- [ ] situation
- [ ] method
- [ ] obvious

2차 복습

- [ ] cotton
- [ ] clothes
- [ ] wool
- [ ] lamb

3차 복습

- [ ] introduce
- [ ] however
- [ ] gesture
- [ ] interact

※ 망각 제로! 1일 전 3일 전 7일 전 학습한 단어를 복습해요.

 **Word Tip**

who 누구	when 언제	where 어디에	how 어떻게
why 왜	situation 상황	method 방법	obvious 명백한, 분명한
cotton 면, 목화	clothes 옷, 의복	wool 모직, 울	lamb 어린 양
introduce 소개하다, 도입하다	however 하지만, 그러나	gesture 몸짓	interact 소통하다

Let's blow bubbles!

Pop Quiz Choose and check the right words.

Kiara blows many bubbles in one breath.

키아라는 한 숨에 많은 비눗방울을 _____ .

- [ ] 소개하다
- [ ] 불다

Dennis can make one hundred bubbles.

데니스는 _____ 백 개를 만들 수 있어요.

- [ ] 액체
- [ ] 거품, 비눗방울

Read & Write Write the **Basic Words** and **Jump Up Words**.

bubble 거품, 비눗방울	**He is blowing bubbles in his milk.** ⓝ 그는 우유에 거품을 불고 있어요. _____ _____ _____

air 공중, 대기, 공기	**The plastic ball is floating in the air.** ⓝ 플라스틱 공이 공중에 떠 있어요. _____ _____ _____

brand 브랜드, 상표	**What brand of detergent do you use?** ⓝ 어떤 브랜드의 세제를 사용하나요? _____ _____ _____

cycle
주기, 순환

They studied the cycle of life in science class. (n)

그들은 과학 시간에 생명의 주기를 공부했어요.

hundred
백, 100개

I want to make one hundred bubbles. (n)

나는 비눗방울 백 개를 만들고 싶어요.

soap
비누

There is soap in the bathroom. (n)

욕실에 비누가 있어요.

blow
불다

The wind blows all day. (v)

하루 종일 바람이 불어요.

liquid
액체,
액체 형태의

Water and milk are liquids. (n)(a)

물과 우유는 액체예요.

A Choose and write the words.

bubble	air	cycle

1

주기, 순환

2

거품, 비눗방울

3

공중, 대기, 공기

B Choose and write the words.

brand	soap	liquid	blow

1 액체, 액체 형태의

2 비누

3 브랜드, 상표

4 불다

C Connect and fill in the blanks.

1

What brand of detergent do you use?

어떤 _____의 세제를 사용하나요?

2

There is soap in the bathroom.

욕실에 _____가 있어요.

3

I want to make one hundred bubbles.

나는 비눗방울 _____ 개를 만들고 싶어요.

D Rearrange and write the sentences.

1 하루 종일 바람이 불어요.

day   all   The   blows   wind   .

_____

2 물과 우유는 액체예요.

and   are   Water   milk   liquids   .

_____

WORD SEARCH Find, circle, and write the words.

museum

j _____

l _____

b _____

c _____

c _____

g _____

s _____

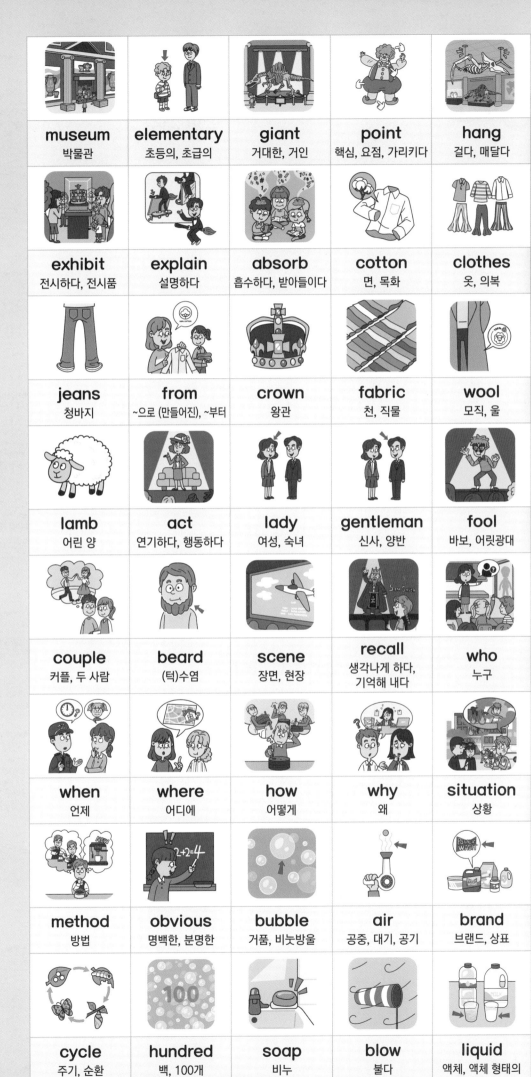

museum	elementary	giant	point	hang
박물관	초등의, 초급의	거대한, 거인	핵심, 요점, 가리키다	걸다, 매달다
exhibit	explain	absorb	cotton	clothes
전시하다, 전시품	설명하다	흡수하다, 받아들이다	면, 목화	옷, 의복
jeans	from	crown	fabric	wool
청바지	~으로 (만들어진), ~부터	왕관	천, 직물	모직, 울
lamb	act	lady	gentleman	fool
어린 양	연기하다, 행동하다	여성, 숙녀	신사, 양반	바보, 어릿광대
couple	beard	scene	recall	who
커플, 두 사람	(턱)수염	장면, 현장	생각나게 하다, 기억해 내다	누구
when	where	how	why	situation
언제	어디에	어떻게	왜	상황
method	obvious	bubble	air	brand
방법	명백한, 분명한	거품, 비눗방울	공중, 대기, 공기	브랜드, 상표
cycle	hundred	soap	blow	liquid
주기, 순환	백, 100개	비누	불다	액체, 액체 형태의

Day 21~25

맞힌 개수 : ☐ / 40

❶ museum		㉑ 걸다, 매달다	
❷ elementary		㉒ 전시하다, 전시품	
❸ absorb		㉓ 설명하다	
❹ point		㉔ 거대한, 거인	
❺ cotton		㉕ 왕관	
❻ clothes		㉖ 천, 직물	
❼ jeans		㉗ 모직, 울	
❽ from		㉘ 어린 양	
❾ act		㉙ 커플, 두 사람	
❿ lady		㉚ (턱)수염	
⓫ gentleman		㉛ 장면, 현장	
⓬ recall		㉜ 바보, 어릿광대	
⓭ who		㉝ 왜	
⓮ when		㉞ 상황	
⓯ where		㉟ 방법	
⓰ how		㊱ 명백한, 분명한	
⓱ bubble		㊲ 백, 100개	
⓲ air		㊳ 비누	
⓳ brand		㊴ 불다	
⓴ liquid		㊵ 주기, 순환	

Answer
Key

Level 3.2

Day 01

P11

 **Pop Quiz** ✓ 세기 ☐ 대학 ✓ 유리 ☐ 평화

P14~15

Skill Up

A Choose and write the words.

history	college	century

❶ century
세기, 100년

❷ history
역사

❸ college
대학

B Choose and write the words.

provide	modern	peace	glass

❶ 평화 — peace / peace

❷ 제공하다, 주다 — provide / provide

❸ 유리 — glass / glass

❹ 현대적인, 현대의 — modern / modern

C Unscramble and complete the sentences.

❶ 그 전쟁은 여러 해 동안 지속되었어요.　a t l s e d
The war lasted for many years.

❷ 이 건물은 유리로 만들어졌어요.　l s s g a
This building is made of glass .

❸ 서울은 현대적인 도시예요.　m r e n d o
Seoul is a modern city.

D Choose and complete the sentences.

history	century	college

❶ 한 세기는 100년이에요.
A century is one hundred years.

❷ 나는 역사를 잘 알아요.
I am good at history .

❸ 이 대학은 1936년에 설립되었어요.
This college was founded in 1936.

14　15

Day 02

P17

Pop Quiz ✓ 미래 ☐ 변호사 ☐ 요리사 ✓ 교수

P20~21

Skill Up

A Find, circle, and write the words.

❶ （future）j h
미래　future

❷ q u（become）
~이 되다　become

❸ k（wish）h e t
바라다, 원하다　wish

❹ e（lawyer）a
변호사　lawyer

B Cross out, unscramble, and write the words.

❶ 도서관　l b a r r y i ~~x~~　library

❷ 요리사　~~x~~ c f e h　chef

❸ 기술자　r g e n i n e e ~~x~~　engineer

❹ 교수　r o r o p ~~m~~ f s s e　professor

C Connect and fill in the blanks.

❶ I want to be a professor.
나는 교수 가 되고 싶어요.

❷ He is a world-famous chef.
그는 세계적으로 유명한 요리사 예요.

❸ He works at a library.
그는 도서관 에서 일해요.

D Rearrange and write the sentences.

❶ 우리는 모두 좋은 직업을 바라요.
wish　good　for　all　We　jobs　.
We all wish for good jobs.

❷ 나는 영화감독이 될 거예요.
I　film director　a　become　will　.
I will become a film director.

20　21

Day 03

 Pop Quiz ☐ 현대적인 ☑ 맑은 ☑ 준비가 된 ☐ 곧

P26~27

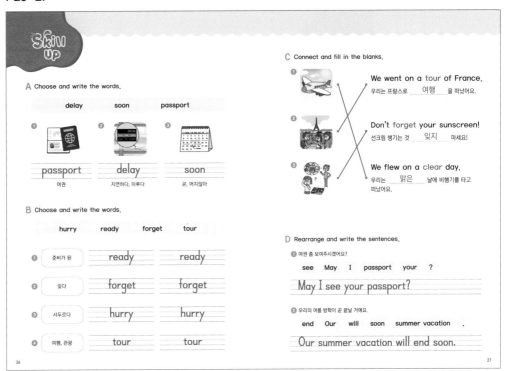

Skill up

A Choose and write the words.

| delay | soon | passport |

① passport
여권

② delay
지연하다, 미루다

③ soon
곧, 머지않아

B Choose and write the words.

| hurry | ready | forget | tour |

① 준비가 된 — ready / ready

② 잊다 — forget / forget

③ 서두르다 — hurry / hurry

④ 여행, 관광 — tour / tour

C Connect and fill in the blanks.

① We went on a tour of France.
우리는 프랑스로 여행 을 떠났어요.

② Don't forget your sunscreen!
선크림 챙기는 것 잊지 마세요!

③ We flew on a clear day.
우리는 맑은 날에 비행기를 타고 떠났어요.

D Rearrange and write the sentences.

① 여권 좀 보여주시겠어요?
see May I passport your ?
May I see your passport?

② 우리의 여름 방학이 곧 끝날 거예요.
end Our will soon summer vacation .
Our summer vacation will end soon.

26   27

Day 04

P29

 **Pop Quiz** ☐ 건조한 ☑ 젖은 ☑ 목욕 ☐ 비밀

P32~33

Skill up

A Choose and write the words.

| shock | decide | apply |

① decide
결정하다

② shock
충격을 주다, 충격

③ apply
바르다, 신청하다

B Choose and write the words.

| strange | dry | bath | wet |

① 이상한, 낯선 — strange / strange

② 마르다, 건조한 — dry / dry

③ 젖은 — wet / wet

④ 목욕, 욕조 — bath / bath

C Unscramble and complete the sentences.

① 내 고양이가 비에 젖었어요.　　t e w
My cat got wet in the rain.

② 우리는 비밀을 지키기로 약속했어요.　　e c r t s e
We promised to keep the secret .

③ 나는 자기 전에 목욕해요.　　t h a b
I take a bath before bed.

D Choose and complete the sentences.

| Apply | shocked | decided |

① 나는 그 소식을 듣고 충격을 받았어요.
I was shocked to hear the news.

② 그는 집에 일찍 가기로 결정했어요.
He decided to go home early.

③ 로션을 얼굴에 바르세요.
Apply the lotion to your face.

32   33

Day 05

P35

 PoP Quiz ☐ 오른쪽 ☑ 왼쪽 ☑ 공공의 ☐ 무작위의

P38~39

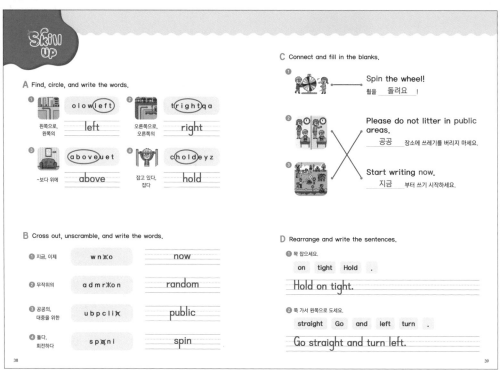

Skill UP

A Find, circle, and write the words.

1. 왼쪽으로, 왼쪽의 — ⓞ l o w (l e f t) — **left**
2. 오른쪽으로, 오른쪽의 — t (r i g h t) q a — **right**
3. ~보다 위에 — (a b o v e) u e t — **above**
4. 잡고 있다, 잡다 — c (h o l d) e y z — **hold**

B Cross out, unscramble, and write the words.

1. 지금, 이제 — w n ⨯ o — **now**
2. 무작위의 — a d m r ⨯ o n — **random**
3. 공공의, 대중을 위한 — u b p c l i ⨯ — **public**
4. 돌다, 회전하다 — s p ⨯ n i — **spin**

C Connect and fill in the blanks.

1. Spin the wheel!
   휠을 **돌려요** !

2. Please do not litter in public areas.
   공공 장소에 쓰레기를 버리지 마세요.

3. Start writing now.
   지금 부터 쓰기 시작하세요.

D Rearrange and write the sentences.

1. 꽉 잡으세요.
   on tight Hold .
   Hold on tight.

2. 쭉 가서 왼쪽으로 도세요.
   straight Go and left turn .
   Go straight and turn left.

Day 01~05

P40

WORD SEARCH Find, circle, and write the words.

Words go in 2 directions →↓

```
h l h t c x u d d w
m b a t h l k q r q
g c x r i g h t m v
l f q c j k r t k l
e u e c e q p o z l
f t c e n r o w b z
t u l n t g o k v u
v r e t u r k d a t
r e a r k d t a u o
y i p y p y i v r r
```

Word Bank
last · wish
century · bath
future · tour
clear · wet
right · left

century | future | last | wet | left
tour | wish | clear | bath | right

P42

Review TEST

맞힌 개수: [ ] /40

❶ history	역사	㉑ 유리	glass
❷ last	지속되다	㉒ 세기, 100년	century
❸ peace	평화	㉓ 현대적인, 현대의	modern
❹ college	대학	㉔ 제공하다, 주다	provide
❺ future	미래	㉕ 도서관	library
❻ become	~이 되다	㉖ 교수	professor
❼ wish	바라다, 원하다	㉗ 요리사	chef
❽ engineer	기술자	㉘ 변호사	lawyer
❾ tour	여행, 관광	㉙ 준비가 된	ready
❿ forget	잊다	㉚ 여권	passport
⓫ clear	맑은, 깨끗한	㉛ 곧, 머지않아	soon
⓬ hurry	서두르다	㉜ 지연하다, 미루다	delay
⓭ dry	마르다, 건조한	㉝ 목욕, 욕조	bath
⓮ wet	젖은	㉞ 바르다, 신청하다	apply
⓯ decide	결정하다	㉟ 비밀, 비결	secret
shock	충격을 주다, 충격	이상한, 낯선	strange
left	왼쪽으로, 왼쪽의	지금, 이제	now
right	오른쪽으로, 오른쪽의	무작위의	random
above	~보다 위에	공공의, 대중을 위한	public
hold	잡고 있다, 잡다	돌다, 회전하다	spin

P45

 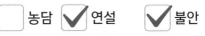 농담 ✓ 연설 ✓ 불안 목소리

P48~49

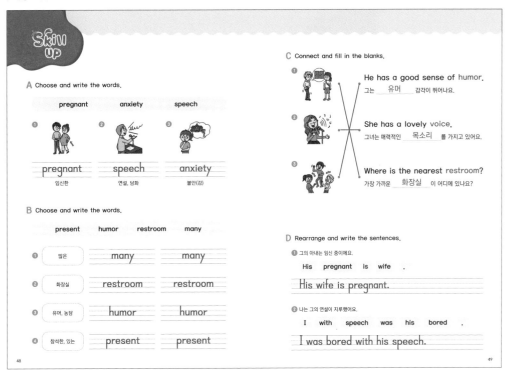

Skill UP

A Choose and write the words.

pregnant	anxiety	speech

❶ pregnant
임신한

❷ speech
연설, 담화

❸ anxiety
불안(감)

B Choose and write the words.

present	humor	restroom	many

❶ 많은 — many — many

❷ 화장실 — restroom — restroom

❸ 유머, 농담 — humor — humor

❹ 참석한, 있는 — present — present

C Connect and fill in the blanks.

❶ He has a good sense of humor.
그는 유머 감각이 뛰어나요.

❷ She has a lovely voice.
그녀는 매력적인 목소리 를 가지고 있어요.

❸ Where is the nearest restroom?
가장 가까운 화장실 이 어디에 있나요?

D Rearrange and write the sentences.

❶ 그의 아내는 임신 중이에요.

His pregnant is wife .

His wife is pregnant.

❷ 나는 그의 연설이 지루했어요.

I with speech was his bored .

I was bored with his speech.

48

49

P51

  ✓ 북쪽 남쪽 ✓ 동쪽 서쪽

P54~55

Skill UP

A Choose and write the words.

bottom	overhead	likely

❶ bottom
맨 아래 (부분), 바닥

❷ overhead
머리 위로, 머리 위의

❸ likely
~할 것 같은

B Choose and write the words.

south	west	east	north

❶ 동쪽 — east — east

❷ 서쪽 — west — west

❸ 남쪽 — south — south

❹ 북쪽 — north — north

C Unscramble and complete the sentences.

❶ 새들이 남쪽으로 날아가요. t h s u o
Birds fly to the south .

❷ 펭귄들이 북쪽으로 수영해요. n o h t r
Penguins swim to the north .

❸ 북극성을 제외하고, 별들은 동쪽에서 떠요. s r e i
Stars rise in the east, except for Polaris.

D Choose and complete the sentences.

overhead	east	west

❶ 해는 서쪽으로 져요.
The sun sets in the west .

❷ 해는 동쪽에서 떠요.
The sun rises in the east .

❸ 비둘기 한 마리가 머리 위로 낮게 지나갔어요.
A pigeon passed low overhead .

54

55

Day 08

P57

PoP Quiz ☑ 부수다 ☐ 용서하다 ☑ 거짓말하다 ☐ 덮다

P60~61

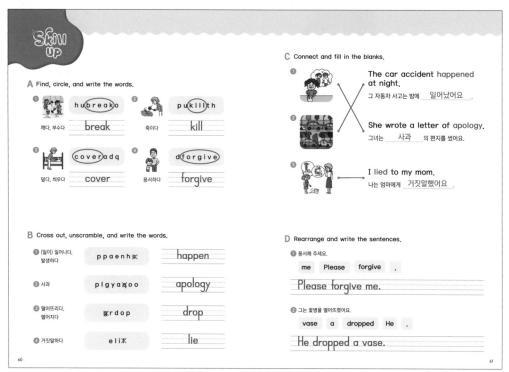

Skill Up

A Find, circle, and write the words.

1. hu(break)o — 깨다, 부수다 — break
2. pu(kill)th — 죽이다 — kill
3. (cover)adq — 덮다, 씌우다 — cover
4. d(forgive) — 용서하다 — forgive

B Cross out, unscramble, and write the words.

1. (일이) 일어나다, 발생하다 — ppaenhx — happen
2. 사과 — plgyaxoo — apology
3. 떨어뜨리다, 떨어지다 — xrdop — drop
4. 거짓말하다 — elix — lie

C Connect and fill in the blanks.

1. The car accident happened at night.
   그 자동차 사고는 밤에 __일어났어요__.
2. She wrote a letter of apology.
   그녀는 __사과__ 의 편지를 썼어요.
3. I lied to my mom.
   나는 엄마에게 __거짓말했어요__.

D Rearrange and write the sentences.

1. 용서해 주세요.
   me Please forgive .
   __Please forgive me.__
2. 그는 꽃병을 떨어뜨렸어요.
   vase a dropped He .
   __He dropped a vase.__

60

61

Day 09

P63

PoP Quiz ☐ 데려오다 ☑ 막다 ☑ 그림자 ☐ 염소

P66~67

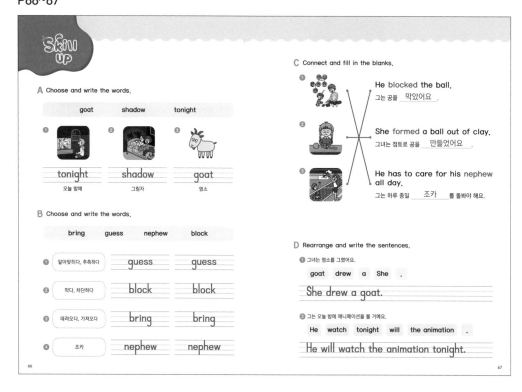

Skill Up

A Choose and write the words.

goat shadow tonight

1. tonight — 오늘 밤에
2. shadow — 그림자
3. goat — 염소

B Choose and write the words.

bring guess nephew block

1. 알아맞히다, 추측하다 — guess — guess
2. 막다, 차단하다 — block — block
3. 데려오다, 가져오다 — bring — bring
4. 조카 — nephew — nephew

C Connect and fill in the blanks.

1. He blocked the ball.
   그는 공을 __막았어요__.
2. She formed a ball out of clay.
   그녀는 점토로 공을 __만들었어요__.
3. He has to care for his nephew all day.
   그는 하루 종일 __조카__ 를 돌봐야 해요.

D Rearrange and write the sentences.

1. 그녀는 염소를 그렸어요.
   goat drew a She .
   __She drew a goat.__
2. 그는 오늘 밤에 애니메이션을 볼 거예요.
   He watch tonight will the animation .
   __He will watch the animation tonight.__

66

67

P69

 Pop Quiz ✓ 폭탄 ☐ 전투 ✓ 땀 ☐ 걸음

P72~73

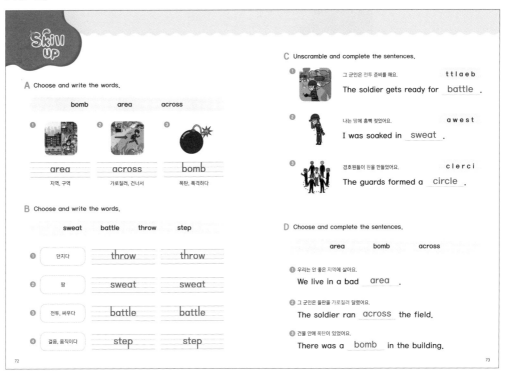

Skill Up

A Choose and write the words.

bomb   area   across

① area
지역, 구역

② across
가로질러, 건너서

③ bomb
폭탄, 폭격하다

B Choose and write the words.

sweat   battle   throw   step

① 던지다 → throw   throw
② 땀 → sweat   sweat
③ 전투, 싸우다 → battle   battle
④ 걸음, 움직이다 → step   step

C Unscramble and complete the sentences.

① 그 군인은 전투 준비를 해요.   t t l a e b
The soldier gets ready for   battle .

② 나는 땀에 흠뻑 젖었어요.   a w e s t
I was soaked in   sweat .

③ 경호원들이 원을 만들었어요.   c l e r c i
The guards formed a   circle .

D Choose and complete the sentences.

area   bomb   across

① 우리는 안 좋은 지역에 살아요.
We live in a bad   area .

② 그 군인은 들판을 가로질러 달렸어요.
The soldier ran   across   the field.

③ 건물 안에 폭탄이 있었어요.
There was a   bomb   in the building.

72   73

P74   P76

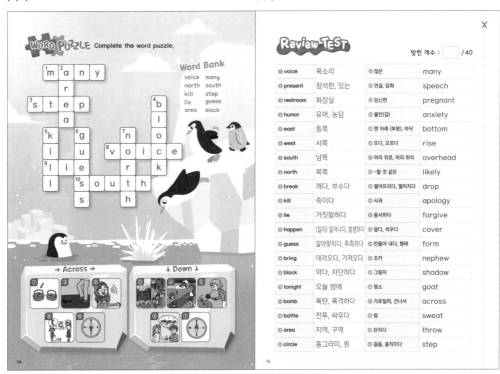

Word Puzzle Complete the word puzzle.

Word Bank
voice   many
north   south
kill   step
lie   guess
area   block

① m a n y
③ s t e p
⑧ v o i c e
⑨ l i e
⑩ s o u t h

→ Across →   ↓ Down ↓

Review Test   맞힌 개수 : ____ /40

① voice	목소리	㉑ 많은	many
② present	참석한, 있는	㉒ 연설, 담화	speech
③ restroom	화장실	㉓ 임신한	pregnant
④ humor	유머, 농담	㉔ 불안(감)	anxiety
⑤ east	동쪽	㉕ 맨 아래 (부분), 바닥	bottom
⑥ west	서쪽	㉖ 뜨다, 오르다	rise
⑦ south	남쪽	㉗ 머리 위로, 머리 위의	overhead
⑧ north	북쪽	㉘ ~할 것 같은	likely
⑨ break	깨다, 부수다	㉙ 떨어뜨리다, 떨어지다	drop
⑩ kill	죽이다	㉚ 사과	apology
⑪ lie	거짓말하다	㉛ 용서하다	forgive
⑫ happen	(일이) 일어나다, 발생하다	㉜ 덮다, 씌우다	cover
⑬ guess	알아맞히다, 추측하다	㉝ 만들어 내다, 형태	form
⑭ bring	데려오다, 가져오다	㉞ 조카	nephew
⑮ block	막다, 차단하다	㉟ 그림자	shadow
⑯ tonight	오늘 밤에	㊱ 염소	goat
⑰ bomb	폭탄, 폭격하다	㊲ 가로질러, 건너서	across
⑱ battle	전투, 싸우다	㊳ 땀	sweat
⑲ area	지역, 구역	㊴ 던지다	throw
⑳ circle	동그라미, 원	㊵ 걸음, 움직이다	step

74   76

Day 11

P79

 ✓ 이미, 벌써 ☐ 매우 ☐ 나누다 ✓ 관리하다

P82~83

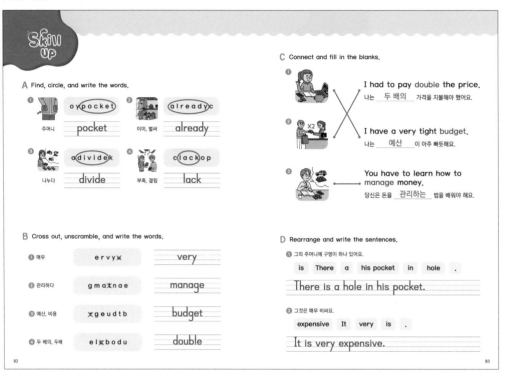

A Find, circle, and write the words.

1. 주머니 — pocket
2. 이미, 벌써 — already
3. 나누다 — divide
4. 부족, 결핍 — lack

B Cross out, unscramble, and write the words.

1. 매우 — e r v y — very
2. 관리하다 — g m a n a e — manage
3. 예산, 비용 — g e u d t b — budget
4. 두 배의, 두배 — e l b o d u — double

C Connect and fill in the blanks.

1. I had to pay double the price.
   나는 ___두 배의___ 가격을 지불해야 했어요.
2. I have a very tight budget.
   나는 ___예산___ 이 아주 빠듯해요.
3. You have to learn how to manage money.
   당신은 돈을 ___관리하는___ 법을 배워야 해요.

D Rearrange and write the sentences.

1. 그의 주머니에 구멍이 하나 있어요.
   is There a his pocket in hole .
   There is a hole in his pocket.
2. 그것은 매우 비싸요.
   expensive It very is .
   It is very expensive.

Day 12

P85

 ☐ 힘 ✓ 냄새 ✓ 정말 ☐ ~보다

P88~89

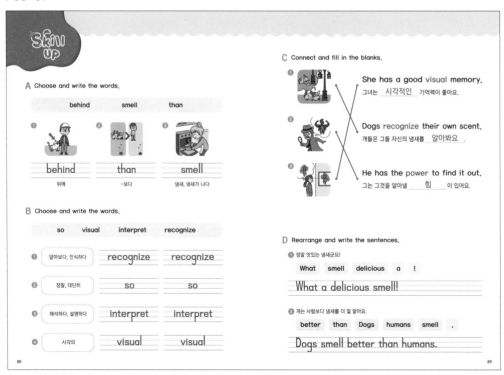

A Choose and write the words.

behind   smell   than

1. behind — 뒤에
2. than — ~보다
3. smell — 냄새, 냄새가 나다

B Choose and write the words.

so   visual   interpret   recognize

1. 알아보다, 인식하다 — recognize — recognize
2. 정말, 대단히 — so — so
3. 해석하다, 설명하다 — interpret — interpret
4. 시각의 — visual — visual

C Connect and fill in the blanks.

1. She has a good visual memory.
   그녀는 ___시각적인___ 기억력이 좋아요.
2. Dogs recognize their own scent.
   개들은 그들 자신의 냄새를 ___알아봐요___ .
3. He has the power to find it out.
   그는 그것을 알아낼 ___힘___ 이 있어요.

D Rearrange and write the sentences.

1. 정말 맛있는 냄새군요!
   What smell delicious a !
   What a delicious smell!
2. 개는 사람보다 냄새를 더 잘 맡아요.
   better than Dogs humans smell .
   Dogs smell better than humans.

P91

PoP Quiz ☐ 금지하다 ✔ 줄이다   ☐ 알아보다 ✔ 동의하다

P94~95

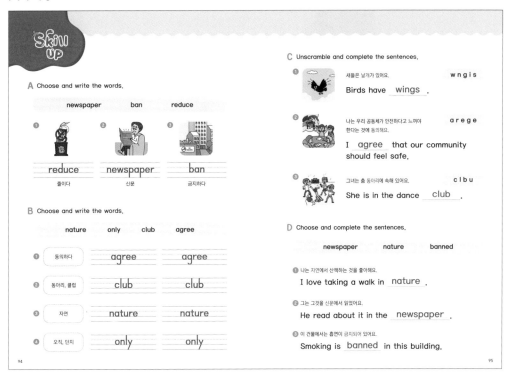

Skill UP

A Choose and write the words.

| newspaper | ban | reduce |

① reduce
줄이다

② newspaper
신문

③ ban
금지하다

B Choose and write the words.

| nature | only | club | agree |

① 동의하다 — agree / agree

② 동아리, 클럽 — club / club

③ 자연 — nature / nature

④ 오직, 단지 — only / only

C Unscramble and complete the sentences.

① 새들은 날개가 있어요.   w n g i s
Birds have __wings__ .

② 나는 우리 공동체가 안전하다고 느껴야   a r e g e
한다는 것에 동의해요.
I __agree__ that our community
should feel safe.

③ 그녀는 춤 동아리에 속해 있어요.   c l b u
She is in the dance __club__ .

D Choose and complete the sentences.

| newspaper | nature | banned |

① 나는 자연에서 산책하는 것을 좋아해요.
I love taking a walk in __nature__ .

② 그는 그것을 신문에서 읽었어요.
He read about it in the __newspaper__ .

③ 이 건물에서는 흡연이 금지되어 있어요.
Smoking is __banned__ in this building.

94 / 95

P97

PoP Quiz ✔ 모험 ☐ 계곡   ✔ ~할 가치가 있는 ☐ 틀림없는

P100~101

Skill UP

A Find, circle, and write the words.

① w o r t h u r e
~할 가치가 있는   worth

② l d x a l o u d
큰 소리로, 크게   aloud

③ n c a l s o a l
또한, ~도   also

④ d c e r t a i n
확신하는, 틀림없는   certain

B Cross out, unscramble, and write the words.

① 헬리콥터   r e t o p c h e i l x   helicopter

② 계곡, 골짜기   l l x e y a v   valley

③ 즐거움, 기쁨   a e p l s x u r e   pleasure

④ 모험   a d v e t r n x u e   adventure

C Connect and fill in the blanks.

① They went on a helicopter ride.
그들은 헬리콥터 투어를 했어요.

② He tells us about his adventures.
그는 우리에게 그의 __모험__ 에 대해
말해줘요.

③ The valley becomes narrower
at this point.
이 지점에서 __계곡__ 은 좁아져요.

D Rearrange and write the sentences.

① 그녀는 그 이야기를 큰 소리로 읽었어요.
the   story   read   aloud   She   .
__She read the story aloud.__

② 여러분은 또한 스케이트를 즐길 수 있어요.
skating   also enjoy   You   can   .
__You can also enjoy skating.__

100 / 101

Day 15

 Pop Quiz ✓ 사탕 ☐ 공장 ✓ 제공하다 ☐ 추가하다

P106~107

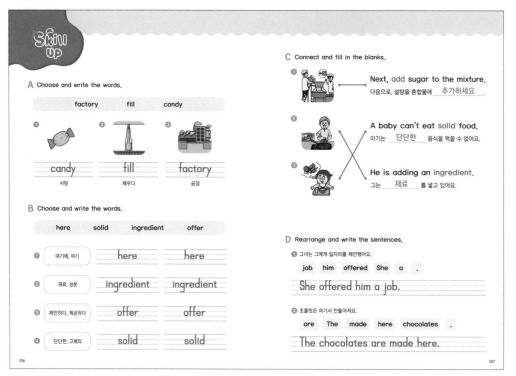

Skill Up

A Choose and write the words.

factory   fill   candy

① candy (사탕)
② fill (채우다)
③ factory (공장)

B Choose and write the words.

here   solid   ingredient   offer

① 여기에, 여기 — here / here
② 재료, 성분 — ingredient / ingredient
③ 제안하다, 제공하다 — offer / offer
④ 단단한, 고체의 — solid / solid

C Connect and fill in the blanks.

① Next, add sugar to the mixture.
다음으로, 설탕을 혼합물에 __추가하세요__ .

② A baby can't eat solid food.
아기는 __단단한__ 음식을 먹을 수 없어요.

③ He is adding an ingredient.
그는 __재료__ 를 넣고 있어요.

D Rearrange and write the sentences.

① 그녀는 그에게 일자리를 제안했어요.
job   him   offered   She   a   .
__She offered him a job.__

② 초콜릿은 여기서 만들어져요.
are   The   made   here   chocolates   .
__The chocolates are made here.__

106

107

Day 11~15

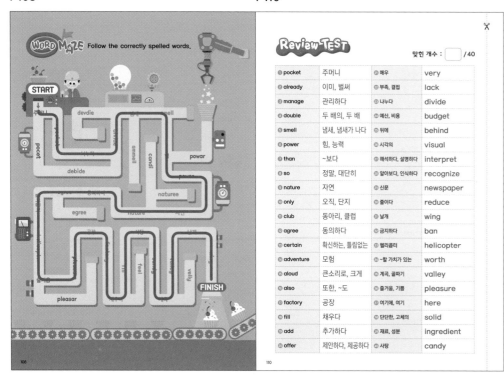

WORD MAZE Follow the correctly spelled words.

106

Review TEST   맞힌 개수 : [   ] /40

① pocket	주머니	㉑ 매우	very
② already	이미, 벌써	㉒ 부족, 결핍	lack
③ manage	관리하다	㉓ 나누다	divide
④ double	두 배의, 두 배	㉔ 예산, 비용	budget
⑤ smell	냄새, 냄새가 나다	㉕ 뒤에	behind
⑥ power	힘, 능력	㉖ 시각의	visual
⑦ than	~보다	㉗ 해석하다, 설명하다	interpret
⑧ so	정말, 대단히	㉘ 알아보다, 인식하다	recognize
⑨ nature	자연	㉙ 신문	newspaper
⑩ only	오직, 단지	㉚ 줄이다	reduce
⑪ club	동아리, 클럽	㉛ 날개	wing
⑫ agree	동의하다	㉜ 금지하다	ban
⑬ certain	확신하는, 틀림없는	㉝ 헬리콥터	helicopter
⑭ adventure	모험	㉞ ~할 가치가 있는	worth
⑮ aloud	큰소리로, 크게	㉟ 계곡, 골짜기	valley
⑯ also	또한, ~도	㊱ 즐거움, 기쁨	pleasure
⑰ factory	공장	㊲ 여기에, 여기	here
⑱ fill	채우다	㊳ 단단한, 고체의	solid
⑲ add	추가하다	㊴ 재료, 성분	ingredient
⑳ offer	제안하다, 제공하다	㊵ 사탕	candy

110

Day 16

P113

 POP Quiz ✅ 대회 ☐ 상품 ✅ 통과하다 ☐ 이기다

P116~117

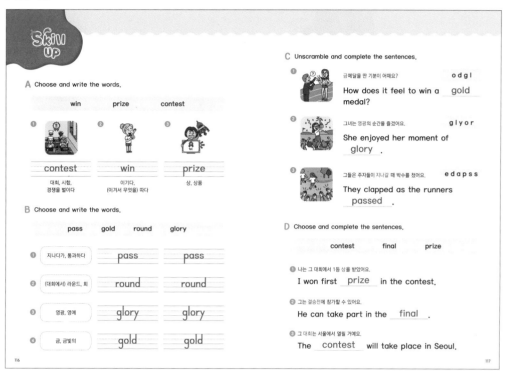

Skill UP

A Choose and write the words.

win   prize   contest

① contest
대회, 시합,
경쟁을 벌이다

② win
이기다,
(이겨서 무엇을) 따다

③ prize
상, 상품

B Choose and write the words.

pass   gold   round   glory

① 지나가다, 통과하다   pass   pass
② (대회에서) 라운드, 회   round   round
③ 영광, 영예   glory   glory
④ 금, 금빛의   gold   gold

C Unscramble and complete the sentences.

① 금메달을 딴 기분이 어때요?   o d g l
How does it feel to win a gold medal?

② 그녀는 영광의 순간을 즐겼어요.   g l y o r
She enjoyed her moment of glory.

③ 그들은 주자들이 지나갈 때 박수를 쳤어요.   e d a p s s
They clapped as the runners passed.

D Choose and complete the sentences.

contest   final   prize

① 나는 그 대회에서 1등 상을 받았어요.
I won first prize in the contest.

② 그는 결승전에 참가할 수 있어요.
He can take part in the final.

③ 그 대회는 서울에서 열릴 거예요.
The contest will take place in Seoul.

116   117

Day 17

P119

 POP Quiz ☐ 종교 ✅ 신 ✅ 천국 ☐ 지옥

P122~123

Skill UP

A Find, circle, and write the words.

① o c exist r   ② religion i
존재하다 exist   종교 religion

③ hell arzi   ④ during fn
지옥 hell   ~ 동안 during

B Cross out, unscramble, and write the words.

① 죽은 사람들, 죽은   g a e d d   dead
② 방식, 방법   y a w p   way
③ 천국, 하늘나라   n v a e e h x   heaven
④ 신   g d e o   god

C Connect and fill in the blanks.

① Do you believe in God?
당신은 신 을 믿나요?

② This is the way we mourn our loss.
이것이 우리의 상실을 애도하는 방식 이에요.

③ Imagine what heaven would be like.
천국 이 어떨지 상상해 보세요.

D Rearrange and write the sentences.

① 당신은 신이 존재한다고 생각하나요?
Do think you exists God ?
Do you think God exists?

② 그들은 돌아가신 분들을 위한 기도를 했어요.
a prayer said for They the dead .
They said a prayer for the dead.

122   123

Day 18

P125

  ☑ 우편 ☐ 사무소 ☑ 돌아오다 ☐ 접다

P128~129

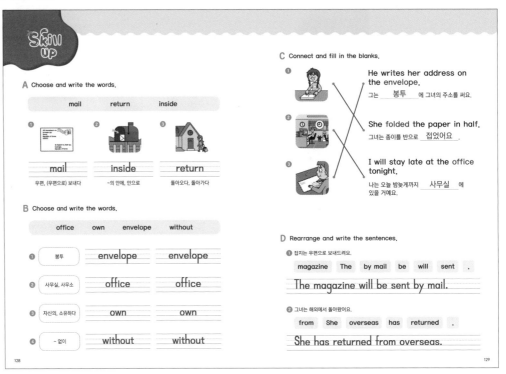

Skill UP

A Choose and write the words.

mail	return	inside

① mail
우편, (우편으로) 보내다

② inside
~의 안에, 안으로

③ return
돌아오다, 돌아가다

B Choose and write the words.

office	own	envelope	without

① 봉투 — envelope / envelope

② 사무실, 사무소 — office / office

③ 자신의, 소유하다 — own / own

④ ~ 없이 — without / without

C Connect and fill in the blanks.

① He writes her address on the envelope.
그는 봉투 에 그녀의 주소를 써요.

② She folded the paper in half.
그녀는 종이를 반으로 접었어요 .

③ I will stay late at the office tonight.
나는 오늘 밤늦게까지 사무실 에 있을 거예요.

D Rearrange and write the sentences.

① 잡지는 우편으로 보내드려요.

| magazine | The | by mail | be | will | sent | . |

The magazine will be sent by mail.

② 그녀는 해외에서 돌아왔어요.

| from | She | overseas | has | returned | . |

She has returned from overseas.

128

129

Day 19

P131

 ☑ 소개하다 ☐ 소통하다 ☑ 수다를 떨다 ☐ 줄이다

P134~135

Skill UP

A Choose and write the words.

gesture	pattern	interact

① interact
소통하다

② pattern
양식, 패턴

③ gesture
몸짓

B Choose and write the words.

however	forever	introduce	company

① 영원히 — forever / forever

② 소개하다, 도입하다 — introduce / introduce

③ 하지만, 그러나 — however / however

④ 회사 — company / company

C Unscramble and complete the sentences.

① 우리의 우정은 영원할 거예요. e e v f r o r
Our friendship will last forever .

② 그는 작년에 회사에서 퇴직하셨어요. p a c m o n y
He retired from the company last year.

③ 두 친구는 저녁 내내 수다를 떨었어요. a h t c t e d
The two friends chatted all evening.

D Choose and complete the sentences.

patterns	interact	introduce

① 그들은 서로 소통할 수 있어요.
They can interact with each other.

② 그들은 행동 양식을 바꾸고 있어요.
They are changing patterns of behavior.

③ 그들은 그 새로운 기술을 소개하고 싶어 해요.
They want to introduce the new technology.

134

135

P137

 POP Quiz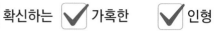

확신하는 ☑ 가혹한 ☑ 인형 우리

P140~141

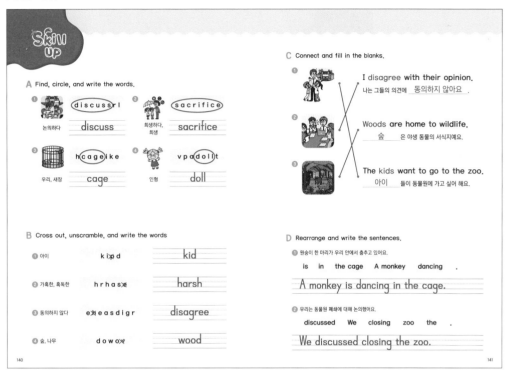

Skill UP

A Find, circle, and write the words.

① (discuss) r l 논의하다 discuss
② (sacrifice) 희생하다, 희생 sacrifice
③ h (cage) i k e 우리, 새장 cage
④ v p a (doll) t 인형 doll

B Cross out, unscramble, and write the words

① 아이 k i p d kid
② 가혹한, 혹독한 h r h a s e harsh
③ 동의하지 않다 e k e a s d i g r disagree
④ 숲, 나무 d o w o x wood

C Connect and fill in the blanks.

① I disagree with their opinion.
나는 그들의 의견에 동의하지 않아요 .

② Woods are home to wildlife.
숲 은 야생 동물의 서식지예요.

③ The kids want to go to the zoo.
아이 들이 동물원에 가고 싶어 해요.

D Rearrange and write the sentences.

① 원숭이 한 마리가 우리 안에서 춤추고 있어요.
is in the cage A monkey dancing .
A monkey is dancing in the cage.

② 우리는 동물원 폐쇄에 대해 논의했어요.
discussed We closing zoo the .
We discussed closing the zoo.

140

141

P142

WORD PUZZLE Complete the word puzzle.

```
        ¹w          ²k
  ³c h a t          i
        y      ⁴g o d
        ⁵w   ⁶r
      ⁷p r i z e
            n   t
        ⁸f       u
  ⁹h o w e v e r
      l         n
        ¹⁰d o l l
```

ACROSS
③ The two friends [ ]ted all evening.
④ Do you believe in [ ]?
⑦ I won first [ ] in the contest.
⑨ [ ], he is shy.
⑩ Do you have [ ]s of different races?

DOWN
① This is the [ ] we mourn our loss.
② The [ ]s want to go to the zoo.
⑤ She hopes to [ ] the gold medal.
⑥ She has [ ]ed from overseas.
⑧ She [ ]ed the paper in half.

142

P144

Review TEST   맞힌 개수 : [ ] /40

① win	이기다, (이겨서 무엇을) 따다	㉑ 금, 금빛의	gold
② round	(대회에서) 라운드, 회	㉒ 결승전, 마지막의	final
③ contest	대회, 시합, 경쟁을 벌이다	㉓ 상, 상품	prize
④ pass	지나가다, 통과하다	㉔ 영광, 영예	glory
⑤ heaven	천국, 하늘나라	㉕ ~ 동안	during
⑥ god	신	㉖ 지옥	hell
⑦ dead	죽은 사람들, 죽은	㉗ 종교	religion
⑧ way	방식, 방법	㉘ 존재하다	exist
⑨ mail	우편, (우편으로) 보내다	㉙ ~의 안에, 안으로	inside
⑩ return	돌아오다, 돌아가다	㉚ 봉투	envelope
⑪ own	자신의, 소유하다	㉛ 접다	fold
⑫ office	사무실, 사무소	㉜ ~ 없이	without
⑬ forever	영원히	㉝ 몸짓	gesture
⑭ company	회사	㉞ 소통하다	interact
⑮ introduce	소개하다, 도입하다	㉟ 양식, 패턴	pattern
⑯ chat	수다를 떨다, 대화하다	㊱ 하지만, 그러나	however
⑰ discuss	논의하다	㊲ 인형	doll
⑱ kid	아이	㊳ 희생하다, 희생	sacrifice
⑲ cage	우리, 새장	㊴ 동의하지 않다	disagree
⑳ wood	숲, 나무	㊵ 가혹한, 혹독한	harsh

144

Day 21

P147

Pop Quiz ✔ 거대한 ☐ 초등의 ✔ 전시품 ☐ 박물관

P150~151

Skill Up

A Choose and write the words.

museum	elementary	giant

1. giant — 거대한, 거인
2. elementary — 초등의, 초급의
3. museum — 박물관

B Choose and write the words.

point	hang	exhibit	explain

1. 걸다, 매달다 — hang / hang
2. 핵심, 요점, 가리키다 — point / point
3. 설명하다 — explain / explain
4. 전시하다, 전시품 — exhibit / exhibit

C Connect and fill in the blanks.

1. Children absorb everything around them.
   아이들은 주변의 모든 것을 흡수해요.

2. The crown was first exhibited there.
   그 왕관은 그곳에서 처음 전시되었어요.

3. The magician explained his magic trick.
   마술사는 그의 마술 묘기를 설명했어요.

D Rearrange and write the sentences.

1. 그들은 지역 박물관을 방문했어요.
   museum They local visited the .
   They visited the local museum.

2. 초등학생들이 현장 학습을 가요.
   go on Elementary a field trip students .
   Elementary students go on a field trip.

150

151

Day 22

P153

Pop Quiz ✔ 목화 ☐ 금 ☐ 왕관 ✔ 청바지

P156~157

Skill Up

A Choose and write the words.

cotton	jeans	crown

1. cotton — 면, 목화
2. crown — 왕관
3. jeans — 청바지

B Choose and write the words.

from	lamb	wool	fabric

1. 천, 직물 — fabric / fabric
2. 모직, 울 — wool / wool
3. 어린 양 — lamb / lamb
4. ~으로 (만들어진), ~부터 — from / from

C Unscramble and complete the sentences.

1. 양털은 따뜻하고 포근해요.   m a L b
   Lamb 's wool is warm and cozy.

2. 이 코트는 100% 모직이에요.   w l o o
   This coat is 100% wool .

3. 이 옷들이 유행이에요.   l o c e s t h
   These clothes are in fashion.

D Choose and complete the sentences.

cotton	fabric	jeans

1. 이 천은 여러 가지 색상이 있어요.
   This fabric comes in many colors.

2. 이 청바지에는 주머니가 많아요.
   These jeans have many pockets.

3. 이 셔츠는 면으로 만들어졌어요.
   This shirt is made of cotton .

156

157

P159

 커플 ✓신사, 양반  장면 ✓여성, 숙녀

P162~163

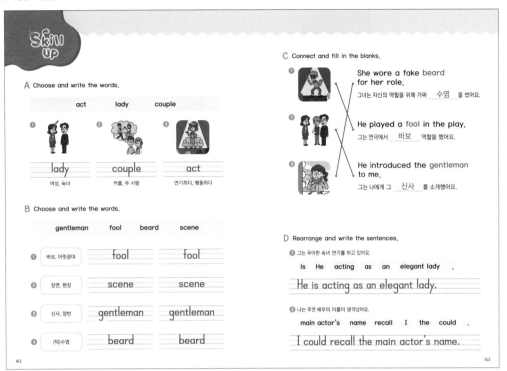

A Choose and write the words.

act   lady   couple

① lady
여성, 숙녀

② couple
커플, 두 사람

③ act
연기하다, 행동하다

B Choose and write the words.

gentleman   fool   beard   scene

① 바보, 어릿광대 | fool | fool
② 장면, 현장 | scene | scene
③ 신사, 양반 | gentleman | gentleman
④ (턱)수염 | beard | beard

C Connect and fill in the blanks.

① She wore a fake beard for her role.
그녀는 자신의 역할을 위해 가짜 수염 을 썼어요.

② He played a fool in the play.
그는 연극에서 바보 역할을 했어요.

③ He introduced the gentleman to me.
그는 나에게 그 신사 를 소개했어요.

D Rearrange and write the sentences.

① 그는 우아한 숙녀 연기를 하고 있어요.
is He acting as an elegant lady .
He is acting as an elegant lady.

② 나는 주연 배우의 이름이 생각났어요.
main actor's name recall I the could .
I could recall the main actor's name.

162   163

P165

✓방법 장면 언제 ✓상황

P168~169

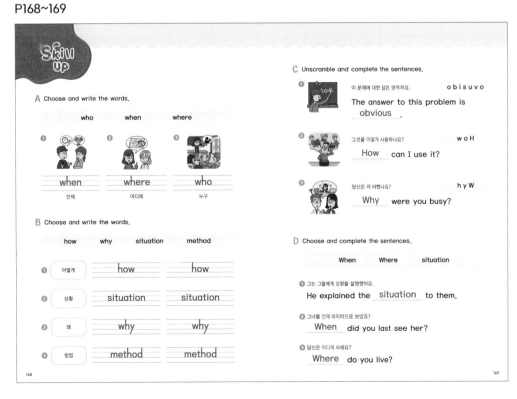

A Choose and write the words.

who   when   where

① when
언제

② where
어디에

③ who
누구

B Choose and write the words.

how   why   situation   method

① 어떻게 | how | how
② 상황 | situation | situation
③ 왜 | why | why
④ 방법 | method | method

C Unscramble and complete the sentences.

① 이 문제에 대한 답은 명백해요.   o b i s u v o
The answer to this problem is obvious .

② 그것을 어떻게 사용하나요?   w o H
How can I use it?

③ 당신은 왜 바빴나요?   h y W
Why were you busy?

D Choose and complete the sentences.

When   Where   situation

① 그는 그들에게 상황을 설명했어요.
He explained the situation to them.

② 그녀를 언제 마지막으로 보았죠?
When did you last see her?

③ 당신은 어디에 사세요?
Where do you live?

168   169

P171

 Pop Quiz ☐ 소개하다 ☑ 불다   ☐ 액체 ☑ 거품, 비눗방울

P174~175

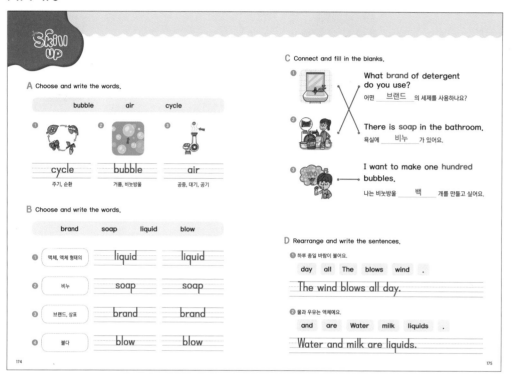

P176   P178

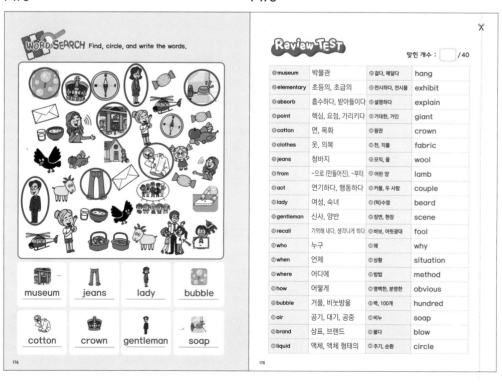

Word List

a

above	~보다 위에
absorb	흡수하다, 받아들이다
across	가로질러, 건너서
act	연기하다, 행동하다
add	추가하다
adventure	모험
agree	동의하다
air	공기, 대기, 공중
aloud	큰 소리로, 크게
already	이미, 벌써
also	또한, ~도
anxiety	불안(감)
apology	사과
apply	바르다, 신청하다
area	지역, 구역

b

ban	금지하다
bath	목욕, 욕조
battle	전투, 싸우다
beard	(턱)수염
become	~이 되다
behind	뒤에
block	막다, 차단하다
blow	불다
bomb	폭탄, 폭격하다
bottom	맨 아래 (부분), 바닥
brand	상표, 브랜드
break	깨다, 부수다
bring	데려오다, 가져오다
bubble	거품, 비눗방울
budget	예산, 비용

c

cage	우리, 새장
candy	사탕
century	세기, 100년
certain	확신하는, 틀림없는
chat	수다를 떨다, 대화하다
chef	요리사
circle	동그라미, 원
clear	맑은, 깨끗한
clothes	옷, 의복
club	동아리, 클럽
college	대학
company	회사
contest	대회, 시합, 경쟁을 벌이다
cotton	면, 목화
couple	커플, 두 사람
cover	덮다, 씌우다
crown	왕관
cycle	주기, 순환

d

dead	죽은 사람들, 죽은
decide	결정하다
delay	지연하다, 미루다
disagree	동의하지 않다
discuss	논의하다
divide	나누다
doll	인형
double	두 배의, 두 배
drop	떨어뜨리다, 떨어지다
dry	마르다, 건조한
during	~ 동안

e

east	동쪽
elementary	초등의, 초급의
engineer	기술자
envelope	봉투
exhibit	전시하다, 전시품
exist	존재하다
explain	설명하다

f

fabric	천, 직물
factory	공장
fill	채우다
final	결승전, 마지막의
fold	접다
fool	바보, 어릿광대
forever	영원히
forget	잊다
forgive	용서하다
form	만들어 내다, 형태
from	~으로 (만들어진), ~부터
future	미래

g

gentleman	신사, 양반
gesture	몸짓
giant	거대한, 거인
glass	유리
glory	영광, 영예
goat	염소
god	신
gold	금, 금빛의
guess	알아맞히다, 추측하다

h

hang	걸다, 매달다
happen	(일이) 일어나다, 발생하다
harsh	가혹한, 혹독한
heaven	천국, 하늘나라
helicopter	헬리콥터
hell	지옥
here	여기에, 여기
history	역사
hold	잡고 있다, 잡다
how	어떻게
however	하지만, 그러나
humor	유머, 농담
hundred	백, 100개
hurry	서두르다

i

ingredient	재료, 성분
inside	~의 안에, 안으로
interact	소통하다
interpret	해석하다, 설명하다
introduce	소개하다, 도입하다

j

jeans	청바지

k

kid	아이

kill   죽이다

l

lack   부족, 결핍
lady   여성, 숙녀
lamb   어린 양
last   지속되다
lawyer   변호사
left   왼쪽으로, 왼쪽의
library   도서관
lie   거짓말하다
likely   ~할 것 같은
liquid   액체, 액체 형태의

m

mail   우편, (우편으로) 보내다
manage   관리하다
many   많은
method   방법
modern   현대적인, 현대의
museum   박물관

n

nature   자연
nephew   조카
newspaper   신문
north   북쪽
now   지금, 이제

o

obvious   명백한, 분명한
offer   제안하다, 제공하다
office   사무실, 사무소
only   오직, 단지
overhead   머리 위로, 머리 위의
own   자신의, 소유하다

p

pass   지나가다, 통과하다
passport   여권
pattern   양식, 패턴
peace   평화
pleasure   즐거움, 기쁨
pocket   주머니
point   핵심, 요점, 가리키다
power   힘, 능력
pregnant   임신한

present   참석한, 있는
prize   상, 상품
professor   교수
provide   제공하다, 주다
public   공공의, 대중을 위한

r

random   무작위의
ready   준비가 된
recall   기억해 내다, 생각나게 하다
recognize   알아보다, 인식하다
reduce   줄이다
religion   종교
restroom   화장실
return   돌아오다, 돌아가다
right   오른쪽으로, 오른쪽의
rise   오르다, 뜨다
round   (대회에서) 라운드, 회

s

sacrifice   희생하다, 희생
scene   장면, 현장
secret   비밀, 비결
shadow   그림자
shock   충격을 주다, 충격
situation   상황
smell   냄새, 냄새가 나다
so   정말, 대단히
soap   비누
solid   단단한, 고체의
soon   곧, 머지않아
south   남쪽
speech   연설, 담화
spin   돌다, 회전하다
step   걸음, 움직이다
strange   이상한, 낯선
sweat   땀

t

than   ~보다
throw   던지다
tonight   오늘 밤에
tour   여행, 관광

v

valley   계곡, 골짜기
very   매우

visual   시각의
voice   목소리

w

way   방식, 방법
west   서쪽
wet   젖은
when   언제
where   어디에
who   누구
why   왜
win   이기다, (이겨서 무엇을) 따다
wing   날개
wish   바라다, 원하다
without   ~ 없이
wood   숲, 나무
wool   모직, 울
worth   ~할 가치가 있는